"So many people have been w[...] understand the personal, emotional, [...] p[...] [...]nsions of these wounds. As a pastor and a professional therapist, Teresa Pasquale is the first person I would go to for help in processing spiritual pain. Now, her gentle wisdom is available widely through *Sacred Wounds*. It is beautifully written and pastorally rich. Highly recommended!"

—**Brian D. McLaren,** Author/Speaker

"In the changing landscape of faith, there are so many men and women across ages, demographics, and faith traditions, lying on the side of the road bleeding. Scarred and hurt from unhealthy systems, many often don't know where to turn or how to find their way toward healing. *Sacred Wounds* is an incredible tool of hope! Teresa Pasquale is an amazing guide, tender and wise, and offers her own experiences, other's powerful stories, and practical, gentle, and meaningful exercises for healing. I will be sharing it with the many people I know longing for hope after experiencing religious trauma."

—**Kathy Escobar,** Co-Pastor of The Refuge and Author of *Faith Shift: Finding Your Way Forward When Everything You Believe Is Coming Apart*

"*Sacred Wounds* is a literary liminal adventure into the holy terrain of trauma, healing, brokenness, and openness. In these pages lie a call for us to be wounded healer-warriors in a fear-ful trauma-saturated culture. May it be so!"

—**Anthony Smith** (Postmodern Negro); Pastor, Mission House (Salisbury, NC)

"Teresa Pasquale's gentle voice of wisdom has never been more needed than it is today. With clinical expertise amplified by a personal journey from victim to survivor to victor, Teresa is the perfect wounded healer, and her words are exactly the balm that all those with Sacred Wounds need!"

—**Reba Riley,** Author of *Post-Traumatic Church Syndrome: A Memoir of Humor and Healing*

"This is the book you need if you or someone you know has survived religious trauma. A definitive guide to the origins of religious trauma, effects on the body and mind, and most importantly, how to heal, *Sacred Wounds* is written by a sensitive therapist and survivor with a full cache of honest, loving, insightful, and creative ideas for how to feel better. Offering illustrative vignettes, therapeutic guidance and practical suggestions for healing processes Pasquale elegantly illuminates the imminent path to recovery."

> —**Michele Rosenthal,** Author of *Your Life After Trauma: Powerful Practices to Reclaim Your Identity*

"The author speaks from both personal and professional experience, and her ideas are well grounded in academic theory. Her writing is both compassionate and full of humor, and tying healing from trauma to the twelve steps of addiction recovery is brilliant."

> —**Gail Horton,** MSW, Ph.D., Associate Professor, Florida Atlantic University

"*Sacred Wounds* is not merely an academic exposé on church abuse. It is both personal and poignant, reaching deeply into the souls of those who are still haunted by the abyss between what we expect church to be and sometimes what it is. This book offers a balm of healing, sacred and pure. Teresa B. Pasquale has heard us. She sees us. She knows us. And she offers us the tools we need to rebuild our lives, our hearts, our souls. This is a brilliant and safe guide through our anxiety, our triggers, our panic attacks, and our nightmares. Reading the stories of those whose wounds are still open, I found myself among them. Each one who so generously shares their stories of healing brings light to all our dark places and reveals the God with whom we are safe. Beautifully written."

> —**Daisy Rain Martin,** Author of *Juxtaposed: Finding Sanctuary on the Outside* and *Hope Givers: Hope is here*

"Teresa Pasquale looks deep within religion's wounded shadows and, like Christ the wounded healer, finds grace and hope there. Her project in *Sacred Wounds* is twofold: to name the traumas in which religion is complicit and to provide a map of the healing pilgrimage. Among the unique features of this compelling work are: individual stories, including Pasquale's, of religion's role in perpetuating wounds;

a sophisticated awareness of body-mind healing modalities; and an application of the twelve-step recovery tradition to articulate a positive way forward for transformation. Pasquale believes the end result of our wounds does not have to be cynical rejection or wounded avoidance of religion, but a maturing ability to 'transcend and include' even the most painful stages of our lives. This compassionate, wise book will help many people."

—**Mark Longhurst,** Pastor and Writer

"Teresa B. Pasquale takes us on her own brave journey—and ultimately, intimately, into ourselves. The spiritual traumas are most sacred. No more averting our eyes. We are gently challenged to look, see, sense. Teresa teaches us to remember and trust our instincts once again. She gives us hands-on applications we can use in our lives. Her book is our guide. Take this pilgrimage with her and emerge transformed."

—**Sharon Daugherty,** Sexual Assault Outreach/SART
Co-Facilitator; Palm Beach County Victim Services &
Certified Rape Crisis Center

"If one of the definitions of trauma is 'any experience less than nurturing,' then life on this planet is daunting, risky business for us frail humans. While the Church can be an agent to bring healing to that trauma, more often than not our religious experiences end up less than nurturing and typically at the hands of well-meaning, yet misguided folks. Teresa B. Pasquale shares with brutal and refreshing honesty her journey in spiritual healing. Hers is not just a story of ongoing restoration, it is one demonstrating that in the midst of the pain, the Divine is there weaving all things into the fabric of a new garment designed to give us and others protection, shelter, and life. As a clinician and healer, the insights she presents bring a bright ray of hope where light is more than ever needed. I am grateful for her voice to those inside and outside of the Church. She is a refreshing change agent who speaks from both clinical expertise and deep, personal experience."

—**Jonathan Benz,** MS, CAP, ICADC, CDWF; Author, *The Recovery-Minded Church*

Also by Teresa B. Pasquale

Mending Broken: A Personal Journey Through the Stages of Trauma and Recovery (2012)

SACRED WOUNDS

SACRED WOUNDS

A Path to Healing from Spiritual Trauma

TERESA B. PASQUALE

FOREWORD BY FR. RICHARD ROHR, OFM

CHALICE
PRESS

ST. LOUIS, MISSOURI

AUTHOR'S NOTE: Some names and details have been changed in the anecdotes of the author as well as in the stories of others hurt by church to protect identities. The content as a whole has been kept intact so that no essential material has been altered.

Cover design: Jesse Turri
Interior design: Elizabeth Wright

www.ChalicePress.com

Print: 9780827235373   EPUB: 9780827235380   EPDF: 9780827235397

Library of Congress Cataloging-in-Publication Data

Pasquale, Teresa B.
Sacred wounds : a path to healing from spiritual trauma / by Teresa B. Pasquale.
— First Edition.
   pages cm
ISBN 978-0-8272-3537-3 (pbk.)
1. Religious fanaticism. 2. Psychic trauma—Religious aspects. 3. Healing—Religious aspects. 4. Psychology, Religious. I. Title.

BL53.5.P37 2015
204'.2—dc23

2015018529

Printed in the United States of America.

For all those
who suffer in silence
and all who speak
their truth out loud.

To the broken wings and the mended hearts,
To the painful endings and the
grace-filled new starts.

You are brave.
You are beautiful.
You are worthy.

"Sorrow prepares you for joy. It violently sweeps everything out of your house, so that new joy can find space to enter. It shakes the yellow leaves from the bough of your heart, so that fresh, green leaves can grow in their place. It pulls up the rotten roots, so that new roots hidden beneath have room to grow. Whatever sorrow shakes from your heart, far better things will take their place."

—Rumi

CONTENTS

FOREWORD

*by Richard Rohr*

Spirituality. Trauma. Openness. These three are so rarely taught together, and so desperately needed. In *Sacred Wounds,* Teresa Pasquale is giving us a gift to weave these together in a three-stranded chord that is not so easily broken.

As a therapist, priest, and contemplative teacher, Teresa Pasquale is vitally in touch with the power of paradox: the downsides of spirituality, the up-sides of trauma, and the beauty and pain that comes from a life of openness in heart, body, and mind. Her work reminds me of my life's vocation as a Franciscan working to reflect some small measure of healing to ourselves and our world.

To keep the *heart space* open, we almost all need some healing in regard to our accumulated hurts from the past. It also helps to be in nourishing relationship with people, so that others can love us and touch us at deeper levels, and so we can touch them. In addition, I think the heart space is opened by "right-brain" activities such as music, art, dance, nature, fasting, poetry, games, life-affirming sexuality, and, of course, the art of relationship itself. And to be fully honest, I think our hearts need to be broken—and broken open— at least once in our lives to have a heart for others…or even to have a heart at all.

To keep our *bodies* less defended…to live in our body right now…to be present to others in a cellular way: This is the work of healing of past hurts, many of which seem to be stored in the body itself as memory. It is very telling that Jesus often physically touched people when he healed them; he knew where the memory and hurt were lodged, and it was in the body itself. Eckhart Tolle rightly speaks of most people carrying a "pain body." Sometimes I fear that most of humanity has suffered from some form of Post-Traumatic Stress

Disorder (PTSD), which reverberates painfully in our legacy of war, torture, abandonment, and abuse.

To keep the *mind space* open, we need some form of contemplative practice, or what those in more Eastern paths call meditation. This has been the most neglected in recent centuries in our Western paths, substituting the letting-go release of genuine contemplation for the mere "saying" of prayers, rote recitation that is a poor substitute for the contemplative mind, often merely confirming us in our fear-based systems.

One could say that authentic spirituality is invariably a matter of *emptying the mind, filling the heart,* and *engaging the body* in one fluid daily practice. It's only befitting a faith that proclaims God inhabiting human flesh, renewing the mind and living from the heart, having a first-person encounter with God and humanity, refusing to settle for second-hand religion.

When Jesus speaks of "the narrow path that leads to life," we want to make it into a dogmatic point about the afterlife. In my experience, it's more of an existential observation of *this* life: wise teachers and reliable paths are *so* hard to find. In *Sacred Wounds* and in Teresa, you have both. Reflecting on her personal trauma and the psychiatric field with tenderness and pastoral concern, Teresa demystifies the mystics, invites us to join in the lineage of contemplative action in the Christian tradition, while finding ways to express hope and healing in our hurt places.

Hurt people hurt people, I've frequently observed. *Sacred Wounds* shows us how to honor our hurts so that we become healing people healing people.

ACKNOWLEDGMENTS

This book is first and foremost for all the voices—the voices of the hurt, the unheard, the invalidated, and the discarded. It is for the forgotten, the neglected, and the negated souls who have been given a false myth of a vengeful God-face and a hateful or vengeful manifestation of divinity. It is for everyone who has survived these experiences, and for those voices in this book of those brave enough to vocalize their suffering for the sake of offering others a resonant story and a hopeful future. I want to pay homage to those voices.

Thank you to everyone who has been brave enough to live his or her own story of suffering and survive it. Thank you to all those persons whose stories populate this book, and the many, many more whose brave stories of hope populate the world—standing in opposition to hate, neglect, and diminishment. Thank you for living your story, for surviving, and, when you can, thriving despite the negative myths of faith.

I want to also thank those wisdom teachers I have found in my own life who have informed my own spiritual journey and sacred wounds healing—and offered me tools and resources to light my own path and help me hold that light up for others. Specifically, a deep thank you to the master teachers of the Living School for Action and Contemplation, including the founder Fr. Richard Rohr (also the generous writer of the foreword for this book), Dr. James Finley, and Rev. Cynthia Bourgeualt. They are mystic wisdom teachers and I am grateful for the years of study at their feet and the lifetime's worth of teachings I have yet to unpack from their knowledge on spirituality, the mystic path, and healing.

Thank you to all those who helped bring this book into being—from those who had late-night conversations with me about the content to those adept hands who helped bring the book into being, from editorial support and investment to cover design and publication. Especially thank you to the wonderful team at Chalice Press—namely Steve Knight, Brad Lyons, Gail Stobaugh, and Mick Silva—who walked through the process of bringing *Sacred Wounds* to life, each and every step of the way.

Thank you to my friends and family who have been amazing supporters, readers, and morale boosters during the late-night writing and editing sessions. Especially thanks to my mother, Patricia Bennett (always my editor-in-chief), and my husband, Christopher Pasquale, who is able to motivate my writing and my life like a shot of espresso whenever I need it, and even more so when I don't know that I need it.

Additionally, I send an immense thank you to my soul sister, Holly Roach, who championing this book before it was even a book, and has been one of the greatest advocates for the *Sacred Wounds* work.

Finally, thank you to my soul mother, Teresa of Avila, who has been the voice in my head that I needed, when I wanted to listen and when I didn't. She walks with me every step of the way, each and every day, and I am forever grateful for her inspiration.

INTRODUCTION

The Human Story, Ad Infinitum

The sacred wounds infinity symbol illustrates that our wounds are inextricably linked to the sacred, and the sacred is inextricably linked to our wounds. Our hurt is the origin of our transformation. As Rumi once reflected, "The wound is where the light enters."

As someone whose life has been peppered with wounds, I can say, definitively that hurt has been the birthplace of the greatest and most transformative places of light entering my life. Most of the time it didn't look that way on the face of it—it always felt like death. But if we study any myth or religious origin story since the beginning of time, we will see over and over again that death is also the midwife to new life. Like the infinity symbol, the journey of life and the spiritual life is not a period or an exclamation point—it is a winding figure eight that constantly feeds back into itself, ad infinitum.

The cracks are where the light gets in.

The pain and suffering of life at its peak can transition to joy. Much like real childbirth, only when the pain reaches a crescendo do we burst into a new place of our own possibility, of infinity, and that crack is where the light gets in.

In therapy, I don't over-divulge about my pains with clients, and in life I don't spend a lot of time ruminating on them. I think part of the benefit of moving through suffering is leaving a trail behind, the crumbs of hope and healing, so others can see it is possible to get better—not just in theory but in reality. I think there is value in exploring our pain and sharing when it is appropriate, so that others can see there is a trail to follow. By no means do I have it all figured out, but I know there is a path to wholeness and healing through trauma, the pain of spiritual disappointment, and other areas of life that disappoint. This book is meant to be a roadmap to that hopeful place—not just created by my own tales of woe and reconciliation, but with the bravery of a multitude of voices who have walked the path of pain and found hope. Let them be a lamplight to the unending journey, so that we might be able to see what is possible for us all.

We are never-ending. We are warriors and creators. We are divine and sacred and worthy. You are worthy without caveat or exception.

Let the story-making and the hope-mongering begin. It is not just the story of me, but the story of us. Welcome to the shared and sacred journey.

Oftentimes, it has been those moments where pain intrudes when I really listen. I've begun to realize a personal paradigm shift is about to happen. I had such a moment standing in the dimly lit room of the yoga studio in Hoboken, New Jersey. I had spent Monday nights there for the last year. Huddled in the small basement with a room of eager 20-and-30-somethings seeking enlightenment from our Buddhist teacher, I sought respite from the painful hypocrisy of my Catholic youth. It wasn't a conscious thought, but it was something like, *If anyone can avoid absolutes and platitudes it's got to be the Buddhists.*

Unfortunately, I was headed for a different kind of awakening—one more akin to the "rude" kind. Yet surprisingly, it freed me from my illusion that only my faith tradition could be hurtful.

I loved my Mondays spent in the candlelight on mats and meditation chairs. The first half was always an exploration of foundational Buddhist teachings, which we all scribbled in our notebooks ravenously. Although many of the students were also students in the yoga teacher-training program, we were all seekers on a quest. The second half was always guided meditation practice. This was where I learned the power of visualizations in meditation to quiet my mind and calm the chaos of thoughts cluttering up my daily life.

So when I bought my ticket to go see the Dalai Lama speak at Lehigh University, nearly a year into my studies with my monastic nun teacher, I thought it would be a proud moment as I asserted my commitment to move into a deeper place of study and investment in the lineage. I remember clearly that we were standing face-to-face in front of the shoe cubby that always sits by the entrance of every yoga studio, and I was taking my shoes out of the cubby to leave.

I had been absent for a few weeks, so she came up and gave me a hug, saying, "It's so good to see you back. We have been missing you."

Feeling guilty for my absence, I said, "I know. Work has been so busy, but I wanted to tell you, I just bought my ticket to go see the Dalai Lama next week in Pennsylvania."

As I completed my sentence, I saw the furrowing of a distressed brow appear on her usually contemplative expression, and she replied, "We will actually be there too. We will be protesting him and his actions. Our tradition disagrees with his actions and engagement in politics. Be careful of his teachings."

Yes. The man who is an international symbol of peace. She was warning me about the Dalai Lama.

I am pretty sure I smiled and nodded and said something that appeared like agreement. I stumbled out of the basement onto the chilly spring sidewalk of Hoboken. As her words settled into my brain, my internal response was something like, "Damn it!" That thought was quickly followed by, "Seriously? No. Not again."

I have since learned, in subsequent years, that the tradition my fairly innocent group of Buddhist, non-Buddhist yogi students were enamored with at the time, the New Kadampa Tradition, seems to be a fairly aggressive and revolutionary group—outside of yoga studio basements in Hoboken. I read an article that went into detail about the tradition and its aggressive actions and for the first time in my life, I felt something akin to a trigger outside of my childhood religion. It was fascinating, but it showed me my church wounds were still fresh, and I was still extra sensitive to fundamentalism, even of a different color—saffron to be exact. So interestingly, the closest I ever came to a cult was in this seemingly benign lecture and practice series in a New York metro-area yoga studio. The irony abounds.

This is not meant to point a negative lens at Buddhism. This experience left me open enough to return to explore my tradition anew, and most importantly, to begin to forgive. This started would bring me full circle and back to the Christian contemplative practices and teachers of my roots. What I found is that no religion is immune to fundamentalism. Religion is made up of humans, and our humanity can be the best of us, or get the best of us.

But this opened my eyes to my sacred wounds and became one of the most profound and powerful moments in my faith journey.

It was like returning to a relationship ended on bad terms to find some kind of closure. I think I knew I would never be Roman Catholic again, but when I went back with a compassionate forgiving heart, it let me explore the good elements of my tradition, rather than throwing them all away as poisoned fruit from the hurting tree (the opposite of *The Giving Tree*). I could see what I loved of my Catholicism with new eyes. By returning, I was granted so many amazing gifts—contemplative prayer, the work of Richard Rohr, a Franciscan monk and mystic, as well as the work of my namesake mystic, Teresa of Avila.

I now think of Catholicism much like a great uncle—it contains wisdom and I love it, but we disagree on a lot. But that disagreement does not diminish my love, and for that I am grateful to my sacred wounds—those that pushed me away and forced me to ask difficult questions of myself and my faith, and those that brought me back to my spiritual home to repair the pieces and begin a healthy, if long distance, relationship.

This is not everyone's story. I have not had the extent of religious trauma many have had, and some of my most acute traumas happened outside of church contexts, so my experience as depicted is just that—my own. I don't expect everyone to go back to their sect or tradition of origin, and I don't expect that to be the healthy choice for many.

We have the choice and the chance to heal our wounds when we want to. It looks somewhat different for everyone. However, hopefully in these pages you will find some space for resonance and understanding, as well as compassion for yourself and others.

The Frontlines of Faith: Suffering, Learning, Loving, and Leaving Religion

I hope this is the beginning of a larger conversation about religious abuse and healing on the other side. The other day a colleague of mine was asked to speak before a domestic violence nonprofit organization. Prior to speaking, she was mingling with people in the gathering crowd, telling them that her area of expertise was trauma and post-traumatic stress disorder. Many responded to this statement with, "Oh, so you worked with veterans?"

As someone who treated veterans for the better part of 10 years, I know the potent suffering of those who've gone to war. Sadly, much of what people know today about trauma is limited to a fairly archaic understanding of trauma and PTSD. Many people still think trauma only applies to war or violent crime, and very little beyond that.

As a trauma therapist I have worked with those suffering from the impact of religious or spiritual trauma. Recent stories of such wounds have come out more extensively. Fingers might initially point at the Catholic Church, yet it is much more widespread than that.

I hope to address abuses in religion where they lie and explain their origins, nature, how they grow, and how we work our way back. Like life, trauma is both more complicated and simpler than we tend to think. Religious and spiritual trauma requires speaking about it. It is pervasive and must be recognized as trauma. The nature of trauma, of religious trauma, case examples, and finding healing must come through a variety of resources and practices to slowly move from hurt into wholeness.

Whenever someone tells me it is *easy* for people to leave church, I think, "You have never met or fully listened to the story of someone wounded by church." People don't leave for a lack of caring. Rather, it's usually caring too much that makes many leave. Most leave with broken hearts. Most leave in mourning. Not all, but enough that it is the rule and not the exception.

These are my people, the spiritually wounded, the soul warriors. If you meet some, be gentle with them. If you are one, be gentle with yourself.

There is no magic secret to faith inside the walls of churches; the people make or break the institution. And sometimes the people in the institution make or break human souls.

The world is sacramental and always unfolding, ad infinitum. Some days finding anything sacred in this hard world is excruciatingly difficult.

I have been ravenous for it all my life—for the sacred in the profane, the glory inside the mundane. There were times in my life I couldn't eat the bread, and so I ravaged a sunset instead. Isn't all food of and from and by God? We must not diminish the sacred in anything; don't diminish the seeking in anyone. This, in itself, is ending an abuse, perhaps one subtler than the overt abuses of religion, but often painful nonetheless.

How many of us truly realize all the ways the sacred has been reduced for us by those who deny it in and around us every day?

This book is my call into the sacred wounds and into the orbits of faith; it is my plea for light in dark places and unconventional lights where more conventional ones have flamed out.

Let us learn the curves of religious trauma; learn the shape of this pain. Abused and abuser, religious and secular, whatever your angle of receiving this information, let it penetrate your mind and search your memory. Let it find your own tiny scars, and trace the outline of their markings to see the world through the lens of this *sacred pain*. Together we can feel it and heal it. Because we heal in community. There is no other way.

I hadn't even finished my first book before this book began demanding to be written. I intended to write it, just not yet. But then the overwhelming need came booming in the midst of everything, everywhere. Wherever I went, I found more people disclosing the stories of their suffering at the hands of Christian communities, church leaders, and faith institutions. The stories resonated with one another like a symphony of suffering. I have studied trauma as a therapist, and the nuances of each story carried a cadence in tune with the one before it, and that story with the one after it.

The stories of suffering could not be swept aside. Soon the book garnered the name *Sacred Wounds*.

The Bible is full of desert wandering and arid landscapes; these are the places of deep suffering and also the most profound transformations. Moses and Jesus, the rock stars of the Hebrew and Christian scriptures (or as some call them, the Old and New Testament), did some of their best work in deserts. The symbol of deprivation, spiritual testing, and excruciating doubt deserts remind me of my darkest moments in faith community. The causes of my own spiritual brokenness were much more palpable in recollection than I thought they could still be, as palpable as sexual traumas in early adulthood (which I talked about in my first book, *Mending Broken*).

To be honest, I had forgotten how painful it was to be without a faith family or home. I had removed myself from the desert and misplaced my visceral understanding of the journey through sacred woundedness.

We are hearty stock, those of us that wander, partially lost, desperately seeking. We cannot be extinguished completely. We understand that deep in our hearts, in a place we may not recognize, the mirages will become real one day and we will find our destination.

I did. For me it was in the Episcopal Church and a community that was safe and means what it proclaims when it says "All are welcome, just as they are."

The way forward looks different for everyone, but I believe at the edge of each spiritual desert there is some place of spiritual redemption, where the hurt is mollified by grace in whatever form it takes. Tonight, in spiritual deserts around the world, there are desert flowers subsisting and sustaining, but without the abundance of full acceptance of love.

The call to the Church and faith communities in the 21st century is to begin intentionally to answer the call of desert flowers—to acknowledge the suffering and the source, and admit that broken people of faith speak to broken faith. There are fissures in our foundation. It may not be in your church; it may not be in your heart, but people in churches are wounding and traumatizing people in churches, and for this we all carry some accountability and some call to respond today.

People inside and outside of church walls are calling to the church to be heard and understood, and for the explanations of why faith hurts as much as it heals.

Not all religious communities, leaders and institutions are hurting people, but enough are that we are all called to respond. We must find our own complicity in this problem. Sometimes it is in our silence, and not hearing or saying the truth. Sometimes it is in blindness, not wanting to see the hurt in others for fear it will touch something that is hurting in ourselves. Sometimes it is in being a hurter because some part of ourselves has brokenness we don't see, and untapped wounds not addressed. Sometimes it is in complacency.

Whatever our complicity, we have to be willing to see and explore that to change the story. We have to change how we are doing things as individuals first and communities second. We must address the spiritual hurts perpetrated every day, or the faith of today will evaporate tomorrow.

The answer to the mass exodus of people from churches into spiritually unaffiliated categories is not better music, marketing, or branding. The answer is deeper than that. The longevity of Christianity as community and institution does not rest on *branding*; it rests on healing.

The answer is less expensive, but more taxing. It is "the pearl of great price." How we respond to this issue today will shape the future of Christianity. This is the prediction (predicated on increasing statistical data that illustrate the same details of religious exodus) of this trauma therapist, lay minister, and crooked mystic.

What is the positive side? We can take back the reverberations of the hurts that haunt us. We can transform the misinformed, angry Father God or denigrating faith community and/or family systems of our origins. We can bring light into the darkest spaces and transform suffering into the kind of hope that only comes on the other side of deep suffering. The bitterness of acute pain impacting the soul changes us. We cannot go back or deny the dark places. What we can do is swim through the murky waters of darkness and into the depths of suffering, face the pain, and come out into a new place—one that we could have never found without pain—one that looks like grace. This doesn't mean the pain is good. It doesn't mean we would have ever chosen it. It doesn't mean we deserved to hurt because we were divined for this particular kind of ache. It doesn't mean it isn't more than we can handle. It just reminds us that we are creatures born for unimaginable resiliency and an unending capacity for hope. It just means we will find our way to the deep sacred center of all things faster than those who have not experienced the acute pain of sacred wounds; and in that process we have been given the secret access to the beauty that is only available to those of us who have lived through pain and know what it is like to be deprived of light, life, and grace for far too long. We stretch toward the sun with an earnestness that comes from knowing how dark the darkness can be. We lean into joy with more urgency because we know the density of a guttural and deep lament. We are a blessed few.—a band of brothers and sisters who do not take grace for granted.

A FOUNDATIONAL PRACTICE: Breathing

When we explore the painful places it can be unnerving. In my work with trauma survivors, as well as in my own life experience, I want to begin with a way to center and ground before I delve into the hurt and broken places. This way if there are tough moments when I feel I might lose my footing, I have a reference point to return to, in order to get my bearings. This grounding practice is like a compass out of the difficult moments and into the present reality of what is in the moment—outside of hurt or overwhelming emotions.

This simple breathing practice is something I offer every person I work with—in both sacred and secular contexts. It is universal because it begins and ends with breath.

Three-part breath is taught in the yoga world, but is inherent to the way in which we are intended to breathe. As babies we breathe in our natural route. When we inhale, our lungs fill with air and expand; when we exhale we pull our stomach muscles in toward our navel, wringing the air out of our lungs. Watch a baby—it happens naturally in infancy. As we grow, learn, and hurt, we begin to absorb a sort of strangulation and reversal of our breathing process. In some form or fashion, most of us adopt a reversal of breath. We begin to inhale and suck inward, and breathe out and push our bellies out. Many, if not most of us, flip-flop breathe at some point in life. There are probably a lot of reasons why, but the many little stresses begin to divert us off our natural breath and into a more constricted way.

For those who have experienced severe stress and trauma, this breath reversal is much more acute. In this way, we begin to feel breathless in much of life. Specifically, in trauma we either hold our breath or hyperventilate. To return to a relaxed place we must begin with the baseline of breath, the anchor of our life. Untethered, we float. Tethered, we are grounded and balanced from the inside out. Soothing and calming three-part breath is the simplest way to correct our learned breathing and return us to the breath of infancy.

1. Sit in a chair or lie down on your back—whatever is most comfortable.
2. Place your hands on either side of your belly.
3. Inhale deeply and imagine that you are filling up your belly with air like a balloon.
4. Feel the balloon filling as your abdomen presses into your belly.
5. When your abdomen is full, pause for a moment then exhale out your nose or mouth.
6. After a few deep breaths, move your hands to either side of your rib cage.

7. Take an even deeper breath, filling your lungs as your belly expands, then your rib cage.
8. After a few deep breaths, move your hands to either side of your upper chest with fingers on your collarbone.
9. Take an even deeper breath, filling your lungs, belly, rib cage, and chest like a wave rising until your lungs are full.
10. Release all the air in a sigh through your mouth.
11. Continue slowly for a few minutes, noticing what it feels like to increase the length of your inhaled and exhaled breaths.

Use this breath practice whenever you feel anxious or triggered. You can do the same practice in any situation without the hands to help calm any anxiety or stress in the body, then the mind.

CHAPTER 1

The Wounds That Bind

The Nature of Trauma, PTSD, and Religious Injury

*My creed is Love; Wherever its caravan turns along the way,
That is my belief, My faith.* —IBN ARABI

I had really wanted to try a zip line; at least that was the reason I remember being so eager to go away to "adventure" camp in Missouri. When I thought of adventure in a camp setting, I imagined white water rafting, treetop obstacle courses, and zip lines. Even though I had a near petrifying fear of heights, I thought this might be a good time to test myself physically—to practice mind over matter.

I should have known, or at least my parents should have known, that when an uber-Christian family from Missouri invites your kids to join them at adventure camp, there might be more than the white water smiles plastered throughout their literature to contend with, in the midst of the Midwestern wilds.

It was not that we weren't an uber-Christian family in our own right. I was raised Catholic, in a long lineage of devout Catholics. I was an adoptee born in Colombia and raised by orphanage nuns for the first months of my life, named by those same nuns after Teresa of Avila. Could you appear to be more Christian? I contend not.

That said, Kamp Kiliki and its campers considered me Christian only in the most marginal sense, since Catholic in some circles can be a dirty word. I didn't really get that. I felt I was learning a whole new world, one in which this overly verbal, inwardly philosophical, and always inquisitive teenager didn't really fit; especially when it came to philosophically questioning. Even back home, I always stood out because of my "use of big words" as others my age would tell me, but at least they weren't judging my worthiness at a cosmic level—only my believability as a 15-year-old. Apparently, not knowing who Madonna was (the singer, not the other one) and, conversely, knowing the works of Jane Austen are not the qualifications for "cool" by teen standards. Here at "Kamp" with a "K," it turns out I was religiously uncool; not irreparably, but definitely not hitting the mark by the cultural standards of Missouri-based "Kristianity."

During this particular sticky summer of 1995, as I fumbled my way through the last lingering moments of preadolescence, my still-developing brain couldn't even fathom how much it didn't know about the many nuances of this umbrella of my Christian faith. I had spent my life underneath its wide-brimmed shelter yew knew so little of its culture and people.

I just wanted to face my fear of heights and try a zip line. But in pursuit of this simple goal, a sequence of life events unraveled with such potency that they would, without any excessive pomp, change the course of my spiritual life. At the very least, they would create a detour into a long and winding "alternate route" of faith.

Billed as an adventure camp it seemed a fairly innocuous, and Missouri a fairly innocuous state (at least comparative to the New York City metropolitan area) and so, in the summer after eighth grade, I excitedly boarded a plane at Newark Airport with my little brother for the "Show Me State," a land of zip lines and whitewater rafting.

Immediately on arrival, I felt the whole thing had a tenor of something else. To be fair, I wasn't at this stage of my life an altogether ideal "joiner." I tried to be kind and hated for people to dislike me (to a nearly pathological extent), but I was shy and not much of a girly girl. I was clumsy and literary. So, in truth I probably would have stood out at any camp, definitely any adventure camp. Add into the mix that this was an Evangelism-style Christian camp with a side of adventure sports, and you have the ingredients for something tailor made for my failure. Add the fact that I didn't even know what evangelism meant at the time, and you have the exact flavor of my kind of crazy experience.

I was a Jersey girl with a penchant for mystic solitudes in what turned out to be the most flamboyant evangelism, amid seven shades of white people, even more white (if possible) than those of my yuppie NYC-adjacent suburbia. They had a special penchant for late night rallies which, if I knew what they were at the time, would have tasted like the flavor of a summer tent revival.

I was in a strange new land, devoid of my Manhattan skyline views and suburban commuter trains, but dripping with sweat and crowded with an overabundance of fir trees. This tribe I had stumbled upon had its own rules, codes, and ethics. The campers dressed in bright colors and were always full of pep, From early in the morning to deep into the night, the sound of megaphones and screeching cheers penetrated the sound system with "praise the Lords" and language I would come to loathe like "believers" and "saved."

I tried my hardest to learn the new cultural mores. Overall it was irksome, sometimes exhausting, severely lacking in the afore-promised adventure, but it wasn't necessarily harmful. It was just really strange to me. I watched their movements, language, and mannerisms. Their sweetness, in contrast to the Jersey-frankness I knew well, seemed as genuine as a hot air balloon filling with steam, corpulent and distended, ready to pop. I wanted to believe it was real—the cheering others on, the friendship bracelets exchanged and exchanged again, and the never- ending supply of hugs.

If you have ever entered a new society, culture, tradition, or religion it is polite and essential to learn the ropes—all zip-line humor aside. So I tried to blend in and smile big smiles, and accept (if not ready to give) big hugs.

Oddly enough, the same over-touchy pep would find me again, later in life in yoga ashrams. Even then, 10 years after the camp, I could never get used to all the hugs. But that's just me.

One of the most surreal cultural mores of this new planet I found myself on was the tradition in which whenever anyone "accepted Jesus into their heart," any time of day or night, they would go with their counselors and ring a bell. That was a thing. That happened.

Even the language confused me immensely. What did that mean? That seemed very esoteric for 12-, 13-, 14-, and 15-year-old girls to be articulating so definitively, as though something like that was so absolute and finite that it could be marked down on a page to the day and time. I didn't get it, but if it made them happy, I figured, "What the hell." Except I didn't say "hell," not even in my head, while on camp grounds. I was pretty sure they had a different bell, maybe something more akin to a boot camp foghorn, if you got caught doing that.

Every night my new tribe on this new planet called Missouri would make their way down to a large fire pit at dusk to sing songs around the campfire. Every day the sing-along began with "Stand By Me," a song I had once loved but learned to loathe from the prescribed monotony of it alone. After the sing-along, everyone from the entire camp, hundreds, maybe thousands of children, would gather in a large auditorium for the bright shirt megaphone proselytizing.

I say hundreds, maybe thousands, because there is a funny thing that happens with memory when it is inflated by pain and time; what might have been 10 people becomes a hundred, and what might have been a high school gym can be recalled as the size of Madison Square Garden. That is how our brain absorbs and makes indelible the things that hurt us; like a drop of ink on a white cloth, it spreads and expands quickly with time. So I can say it was probably at least hundreds, but the only recollection I have now is the indelible ink of memory—foggy in places, absurdly clear in others.

On this night they revisited their poppy rendition of "Stand By Me," like a pied piper serenade as all the camp kids made their way into the crowded hall, many of them shouting and singing along. Hugging and smiling ensued as everyone got all pep-rallied up. The energy was so high in the space I could feel the floor rumbling beneath me, a rhythmic mix of the overly cranked speaker system and the pounding of many dancing feet.

The night's lesson was on heaven. This is the moment when the older me interjects with an all- knowing anticipatory groan, knowing this is where it is about to go off the rails. Barely teen me, naive to the ways of this culture, didn't see it coming.

The camp patriarch, a nearly middle-aged white man, dressed all-too-coolly for his years, stepped up to the microphone and said something I could barely hear to which the whole crowd surged with a high-pitched "Amen!"

He began speaking of worthiness and eternity. He spoke of salvation and being saved. He spoke about who would enter heaven at the end of their lives and the end of time and who wouldn't. Short version: Everyone in the room was in, and probably their parents, but everyone else was by no means a lock. Definitely anyone who didn't believe in the Patriarch's exact version of how it would all go could forget about even trying at the door.

I had never heard anyone talk so absolutely and with such certainty about something that had always seemed to me a determination far above my cosmic pay grade. I didn't get it. I was baffled, and as the crowd surged with applause and I was rocked by the shaking ground full of the urgency of hundreds of pounding feet, I started becoming more than a little freaked out.

Where was I? What was this all about? Why did I feel further from God than I ever had been before in my life? Why did I suddenly feel so far from home?

Inside of that welling fear was something like adolescent frustration and maybe a tinge of indignation. I was offended on behalf of the God I had grown to know in my life. I had also been coded with a learned justice-seeking, born from a mother who weighed strongly in my mind and who had always reminded me throughout childhood to speak out when no one else would for those unsaid injustices and truths. That, and I was innately and inherently stubborn. It led me to question the unquestionable in all situations.

What about the Gandhis? I was marinating in my thoughts, deeply imbedded in my curiosity-laced frustration. as my two cabin counselors and cabin-mates walked back to our screened-in bunks following the rally. Because I was too young and naive to know any argument with this premise in this context was unwinnable before it even started, I heard the question leaving my lips: *"But what about Gandhi?"*

Everyone, simultaneously, looked over at me as if they had all gone partially deaf. For a second that seemed like ages there was a pause, until counselor #1 responded, "What did you say?"

"What about Gandhi? I mean, if what you are saying is true, what happens to all the good people who aren't Christian?" The second counselor stared me down, "Didn't you listen tonight? They go to hell."

This was said as a matter of fact. Even a murderer headed for death row has a jury take longer to dole out a sentence. "But that doesn't make any sense," I persisted foolishly, "You are saying that if someone is a serial killer and becomes Christian before they die, then they go to heaven, but Gandhi doesn't? Just like that?" The counselors answered in unison, "Yes."

"I mean, I don't have a problem with the criminal going to heaven, but I can't believe Gandhi wouldn't be there too." The silence between our sentences was so acute you could hear each leaf that rustled and each bit of dirt that was trodden.

"Teresa, you have to believe this. This is what Christianity means and this is what Jesus said. If you don't believe this then you aren't a true Christian. If you don't believe this then you haven't truly allowed Jesus in your heart. You have to believe this. If you don't, well you just can't call yourself Christian."

This was the moment. This was the moment my heart broke. I had never even considered that there were disqualifying factors to my goodness and Godness; I didn't know there was fine print that was non-negotiable. I wasn't even sure I believed the ultimatum but just the shred of that possibility, that I could not really be Christian slipped into my consciousness and could not be unwritten.

But I was stubborn. I figured if I was going down with the ship I might as well go down fighting for what I believed, even if, as it turned out, what I believed and who I was wasn't really Christian anymore.

I wanted to do what felt right—even if this experience and the answers given to me led me, in the years that followed, to question everything I inherently believed was true about God and faith and Christianity.

So I persisted.

"Well I don't believe that. I don't know what that says about me, but I won't believe that good people go to Hell. That is not a God I would believe in; one that would let that happen."

The silence began to feel eternal, and the distance between me and the others in the group widened with each step, until I felt like the dark might swallow me up. I felt like I would be lost forever in those Missouri woods.

At this point, the gaggle of girls following the counselors step-for-step began to move even farther away from me like a slowly receding wave; these girls who had called me friend and sister just a bonfire, a zip-line, and two friendship bracelets ago. I was carrying some foreign germ nobody wanted to catch; as if this kind of radical cosmic inclusivity could be caught like a cold or the stomach flu.

They knew from the tones in the counselors' voice that they did not want to catch whatever aberration I had. It meant alienation, isolation, and possibly the eradication of God's love and happy heavenly home for all eternity. This was no light sneeze.

And, from what little I knew about the rapidly disintegrating conversation, this was definitely no way to end a pep rally. In the matter of half a mile and a few short words, I had unraveled their pep and was slipping into a potential pit of eternal damnation.

As we reached the cabin doors, the girls all rushed inside and away from me. The counselors instructed them to get ready for bed, letting them know that we (meaning me and the two counselors) would be out on the porch for a while.

For what felt like all night but was certainly a couple of hours or more, I was sucked into this void of competing eternities. The counselors repeated more of the same conversation and I did as well— they tried to save my soul and pull me back from my dance with damnation. We both refused to budge.

By the end of the night we, both sides, gave up from exhaustion. They felt the defeat of my un-rung bell for Jesus, and I felt the wave of indecision, not certain I wanted to have anything to do with Jesus if these were the kind of people he hung out with and these are the kind of ideals to live up to.

I wanted to do what was just, even if it rescinded my all-access pass through the pearly gates. While I can be flip about it now, in the moment it genuinely felt like, based on their night-long interrogation, that those were the options.

Part of me thought they were insane. Another part of me felt as if I might have just given away my Christianity for my conscience. I felt lonely on the porch and for the rest of camp.

Friendship bracelets and hugs kept flowing, but my cabin-mates and I knew we were on different sides of a very thin line. After this, the minutes, hours, and days at camp served to build and well up in me hate for everything they did and stood for in relation to myself. Every moment felt disingenuous. It was only meant to bolster those on the inside of their version of faith, and there was an exclusion for all those (especially myself) who fell outside of their indoctrination.

I never quite believed the Patriarch, the counselors, or the girls who thought I had acquired some kind of cosmic cooties, but I didn't entirely disbelieve them either. I thought if this was truth, then I was outside of it—all happening at a really young age to imagine life outside of a perceived cosmic truth. It made me lonely, but it also made me very angry. I was angry that the vision I had of God, born somewhere deep inside in unending love, had been torn open and broken apart. I was angry that what they were saying wasn't true, about Christianity being this alienating belief system, and that they were perpetuating a lie. I was equally angry that it was a system of alienation, isolation, and bigoted negation, and that perhaps that indwelling face of God I had loved since I could remember was just a myth of my own invention.

I spent decades festering with hate. The girl I was got older and became pubescent and pimply, a high school graduate and retail worker, and a woman leaving home for the Colorado Rockies, but all the while I carried my festering hate with me. I hated the campfire girls and their fleeting promises of friendship, quickly lost. I hated the camp counselors who isolated and bullied me for that long, lonely night. I hated the pep rally leaders and the camp patriarch and all of their megaphone chants. I hated the song, "Stand By Me."

I hated. I hated. I hated.

That hate, born on a sticky hot summer night in 1995 fueled me for over a decade. I ran fire hot on that gas; I charged toward anything standing in opposition of my Christian roots and anything I wouldn't want to share in a confessional booth.

I ran. I ran. I ran.

At the end of the line, exhausted by fighting, beleaguered from running, I was tired of my spiritually homeless runaway life. I knew I had to face the demons created that night. I had to stop running. I had to stop hating. I had to stop holding everyone, including myself, up to a divine barometer that no human could ever equal.

What I needed to convert was not my "wrong" theology, as the counselors would have liked in that long cabin night, but my broken, bent, and anguished heart. Getting right with God and myself meant going back to the cabin and seeing everything and everyone for what they were in that moment.

Those girls were scared preteens, just like me, taught to abide by an ethic I was betraying. They were taught there were divine penalties for any aberration from their teachings. As girls like myself, their fears were proportional to their understanding of the world. Those teen counselors were girls too; only older than I by a few inches and bra sizes. They were doing what they thought to be right. Those camp leaders, with their megaphones and simple alluring pep ... well, we will deal with them a little bit later in the book. The accountability and clemency on this one is a bit more complex, and relates to the larger continuum of this story—the nature of wounding and healing.

The crux of the intention behind returning to the scene of my scarring, back to the cabin years and miles of rage later, is part of a process often used in trauma therapy. We return to the places of our deepest wounds when we are ready, to see the scene with new eyes; in my case. the preteens, teens, adults, and even myself.

On the other side of hate, through the eyes of an adult me, one seeking healing and ready to let go of the years of spiritual baggage, I could see the vulnerability in everyone. I could see the fear. I could see the good intentions even in the wake of bad actions.

It doesn't eradicate accountability. It doesn't eliminate the imprint of hurt it left on my heart. It just allows me to see the humanity in the whole experience, and through my humanity to let go of my resentments. It allows me to let go of the hold the past carries on my present. It allows me to see people with the empathy and kindness I wish I had been shown that night and on others like it, where religion was branded on me like a ranch hand cattle, instead of a warm blanket and loving embrace.

This is the means that helped me find my way back from hate and resentment. This is the path that stopped me from running and let me stare my past in the face, unafraid and no longer bitter.

This is a template to the ways in which we can all, at our greatest potential in our shining moments, deal with everyone we disagree with theologically, philosophically, and religiously.

This is the blueprint for a future built on healed and hallowed grounds, rather than emotional battlefields and rubble-filled churches.

At one time or another, we have been the abuser, the person so certain of our truth that we would mock and demean any other variation. At one time or another, we have been the abused, diminished and negated for speaking or being our own truth. We all need the healing and penance.

Reflecting on my pre-adolescent spiritual experiences and

wounding at "Kamp" does not mean this experience by itself formed my annexation and isolation from church culture. There were other instances. Over time, there were other spiritual slights, hypocrisies, and inconsistencies added, log by log, to the fire of my own rage and indignation.

I tell the story above because it articulates the beginning of my doubt in Christianity and my frustration with human beings in human religious institutions, and it marked the first step in a decade of jading and disillusionment with Christianity.

This is the experience that begins my own path of spiritual fragmentation and empathy for all those who wander spiritually. I tell the story because it is a too-common tale. I hear many stories of religious wounding as a therapist and minister for spiritual seekers and the spiritually wounded, and as teacher of the mystics and mystic traditions. Sadly, my story did not happen in a vacuum limited to that camp and night in Midwest America.

I made a pact with myself on my road back to love, hope, and faith in Christianity (on my and its best of days) as a two-pronged promise:

• Never again would I give an institution the deed to my faith. I found I could participate in a system, without the system itself owning my beliefs, my heart, or my soul.
• I would never let one human's words ever have tyrannical rule over my soul.

I have found that as long as my faith—personal, fragile, and vulnerable—is not run by any institution or people group, then my heart can stay focused on God, Christ, and Holy Spirit, and I can take human fallibility for what it is (mine and others)—a necessary ingredient in the journey, even and especially when it hurts. As long as I kept these promises to myself, I knew I could exist within my religious context and my Christianity without any one experience or person taking down the private altar of my sacred place.

Trauma, Up Close

Trauma is anything that injures the self—the heart and the soul. This may not be the diagnostic definition, but it is certainly the one I have encountered most often when seeing the wounds of trauma in the eyes of the thousands of people I have treated in both secular and sacred contexts who have experienced wounds that reverberate in the whole self.

Sadly, clinical definitions always pale in comparison to the real-life experience of any whole-person malady. Trauma is hurt that we feel from the tips of our toes to the top of our head—it hurts everywhere. When we think of traumatic experience in this context, there is almost nothing that can be negated as trauma. It is all up to the personal perception and is entirely subjective. Who are we, whether doctors or clinicians or any other helping professional, to be the determining factor in how deep or authentic a wound is felt by another person? You define trauma and traumatic stress for yourself. I can give you scales and measures to quantify your hurt, and these can help, but ultimately, hurt is beyond measurement and trauma beyond scientific calculation.

That being said, I will offer some parameters so you might discern your own hurt in the context of traumatic experience. Before we go into any of the semantics, I want to validate your hurt. If you have been negatively impacted by others' actions or the experiences you had inside a religious or spiritual context, I am so sorry. I am terribly sorry the places, spaces, and faces who were supposed to show you the ultimate expression of love showed you something negating. Any institution or belief system that does not value who you are as a person deserves to be scrutinized, because the reflection of love you have been given has been tainted by all the worst parts of humanity—fear, narcissism, neurosis, paranoia, and aggression. If your experience of religious constructs has negated who you are as a person—be it your gender, your sexuality, your life choices, or your independent thinking—I am so sorry.

While I can't know the particulars of your pain, I know the pain of negation, abuse, and hurt, through both the personal and professional lenses of my own life. I am so sorry that you carry that hurt in your heart. It is a heavy, often isolating, and sometimes deadly burden. I am so sorry you have had to experience this pain. I am even more sorry if you had to handle it alone until now.

Part of this book's intention is to create a forum to give voice to religious hurts and wounds, to explore their nature, and to validate the often silent suffering of so many. It is also to give professional validation of this personal wound, and to provide the beginnings of the road back from this hurt.

The DNA of Trauma

Trauma is in the eye of the beholder. While some myths about trauma needing to fit a certain set of criteria still linger in and around the field of psychology and traumatology (the study of trauma and the practice of trauma-conscious interventions), more and more therapy professionals and laypersons are finding agreement that trauma is a subjective concept. What is acutely painful to one person does not inherently carry the same weight of suffering for someone else. This wider definition of traumatic experience also allows us, in the traumatology field and beyond, to look at the world of trauma through a much wider lens.

As it relates to the experience of emotional, psychological, and spiritual pain of what we call sacred wounds or spiritual injury, trauma in a religious context can be seen as any painful experience perpetrated by family, friends, community members, or institutions inside of a religion. Often religious injury can happen at all levels of human relationship, which may be one of the reasons it is so powerfully damaging. One's own family, friends, community members, and institutions simultaneously can perpetuate it. From sexual abuse to negation of one's own identity (as a woman, a gay person, etc.), trauma inside of religion is often perpetrated simultaneously by one individual, and often the community group or institution at the same time.

A simple (but painful) example is a person who is found out to be LGBTQ inside of a fundamentalist religious tradition, which sees queer identity as a flaw, failure, or even sin. The institution created the dogma, the community perpetuates this belief, and often a person's own family and friends enforce this belief and force this shaming ideology onto their loved one. Perhaps the most difficult part is it is often done in the "best" interest of the person who is being hurt and traumatized. This is also perhaps the hardest and most intractable part of religious wounds—that the perpetrators believe in the "rightness" of their hurtful convictions to the far reaches of omniscience and back.

Finally, however, people who have been wounded, those who have a history with wounding traditions or dogmas, and the general public are able to see this kind of injury for what it is, true trauma that often manifests into post-traumatic stress disorder (PTSD). For any trauma survivor, there is a potential for the traumatic experience to get "stuck" in which case it moves from a lived experience into a condition known as PTSD. General study data shows that about 20 percent of people who experience trauma will experience PTSD. That being said, due to the underreporting of traumatic issues (sometimes because people don't believe their traumatic pain qualifies as trauma and other times just because of the inherent shame in much of the pain of PTSD), it is difficult to calculate the exact percentage of traumatized people who experience PTSD.

Additionally, due to the fact that there has been no comprehensive study of religious or spiritual trauma and abuse or its vast spectrum of injuries, there is no way to know how many people who experience this kind of hurt will develop PTSD. Anecdotally, however, from my own study of the experience and stories of religious hurt in the last couple of years, I would say that very few of the people I have spoken with haven't experienced some variety of traumatic stress, anxiety, and depression related to their wounds.

Part of the intention of this book is to give voice to those who have been hurting for years, often afraid of alienation, annexation, or worse, harm to themselves or their loved ones, related to speaking up about their traumatic experiences. Another impetus for this book is to let people know, both those who have experienced religious trauma and those who have not, that this *is* a valid form of traumatization. For reasons we will explore in some of the forthcoming chapters, there are a variety of reasons why this kind of trauma is very complex and deeply devastating. If you have been suffering from this kind of hurt, you can know from this moment forward that your hurt is valid and as deeply traumatic as you feel it is. Your experience is valid, and your hurt is real. Additionally, as we will explore in future chapters, there is also real potential for a path toward healing and a spiritual or moral journey through pain into something like freedom, hope, and joy. As real as your pain is, so equally is your potential to heal. If you choose to seek it but are not ready for the healing journey, then that is ok, too. We all heal in our own time, and we all have the autonomy to choose not to go down that path. I want you to have the autonomy to say, "no," as it is likely if you have moved through the experience of religious trauma or any trauma, then "no" has not been a word accessible to you for too long. This book is a journey. It is an option. It is a choice. You decide what to do with it and how it might serve you.

With the increased understanding in the field of psychology as to the depth and breadth of trauma and posttraumatic stress disorder, there are also a few other concepts that have appeared that are important to understand at the beginning of this journey, so as to better see the path to healing and wholeness. Healing begins with understanding. I have found that to be true in my own journey from hurt to healing, out of my own traumatic experience and PTSD, and with the hundreds of clients I have worked with over the last decade walking that same path. Information is great power. So at the beginning of this book, I offer you the resources of knowledge about trauma, its many versatile facets, religious trauma specifically, and what science and therapy professionals are beginning to understand about traumatic experience that is providing a wider pathway to healing and wholeness.

The Different Dimensions of Traumatic Experience

Traumatic response is a complex set of responses of the body and brain systems working together with the best of intentions. When they work for us, or as they were intended, our body and mind seek to protect us from danger. In our prehistoric lives, that danger would have been very real and physically immediate. In this way, the origin of our traumatic response system is much like our animal brethren. The example I use most frequently is a prey animal in the wild. Imagine a deer in the forest. It has to become alert when sounds immediately erupt in the distance and be prepared to freeze or flee at a moment's notice. In much the same way, our body and brain respond to perceived danger in the same way. We are training from our internal system outward toward a variety of responses—fight, flight, freeze, or submit. In recent years, one additional method of response has become more visible as well, perhaps a manifestation of the complex human nature toward compassion. It is called tend-and-befriend. We will go into further detail for each of these responses shortly, but when activated appropriately and when there is real danger in our lives, these survival responses helps us to respond in crisis situations.

When this survival response is over-stimulated—when it experiences a single or multiple incidence of trauma—it becomes stuck, like a light switch that has been turned on and then jammed in place. When this happens, the brain and body can't distinguish between an immediate threat and a previous threat because the survival response addresses safety and danger from the same overstimulated stance. We will explore in the chapter ahead the many ways this manifests in a person, but simply put, traumatic stress and PTSD become the survival response stuck in place. Part of the process of healing from trauma, religious or otherwise, is understanding the mechanisms that create trauma in order to begin to rewire the stuck system.

Traumatic Survival Responses

Fight is the body and mind responding to danger (or perceived danger) by engaging with it with violence or aggression. This could be nonverbally, verbally, and/or physically. In working with combat veterans, I saw this response in overdrive often; my clients who exhibited this regularly were seen as aggressors but, in truth, in PTSD the person often sees danger everywhere so, unconsciously, their fight response is just that—a response to a perceived threat. Like all trauma responses, this can be worked on, reduced, and even eradicated, but understanding the response and its source is important to beginning to rewire the brain/body system. In religious trauma I see this in the pessimistic or aggressive (usually verbal or written) way people react to others in faith communities. But again, if this is coming from a place of trauma, it is a reflexive response to perceived danger.

Understanding this mechanism as a response to perceived threat is crucial to changing this response for the survivor. For those responding to the emotionally and spiritually wounded person, it is essential to understand and begin to act from a space of empathy, sensitivity, and patience rather than from a mutual stance of attack.

Flight is the body and mind response to danger (or perceived danger), which manifests as some form of escape from the dangerous stimuli. This could be literally fleeing like we would if we were being chased by someone and we ran the other way, or a more nuanced and subtle flight when a person emotionally escapes or creates barriers to relationship with others. Flight in religious trauma can manifest in a variety of interpersonal ways. It might be seen in someone who moves through a large variety of traditions or religions after leaving the faith community that hurt them and who may vacate a new community when there is perceived danger or hurt experience on the horizon. It could also manifest as a general avoidance of religious contexts or in a pattern of leaving or extracting themselves from discussions or persons related to religion. The difficulty of this process is that a person is not able to stay still long enough to find out if a place, person, tradition, or community group has positive and trustworthy qualities. It can become a constant state of flight, which is both exhausting and doesn't allow for the ability to deepen into practice, relationship, or community.

For the survivor to understand this phenomenon means there is a possibility, when ready, to test one's threshold for staying still long enough to determine the difference between actual and perceived danger, and to tolerate some level of difference and conflict, which exists everywhere, as a way of learning to build more complex and rich relationships with people and communities (sacred or secular). For those not wounded—rather than minimizing the hurt and seeing the avoidance or "bouncing" from groups and traditions as some flaw of superficiality and lack of depth— they can understand it for what it is, truly deep hurt manifesting in a fear response. The last thing we should ever do with someone's fear response is invalidate and minimize it. Once people can learn to approach those fleeing faith spaces differently, dialogue between faith spaces and the wounded could be possible.

The *freeze* response as a survival mechanism is often physicalized, but it can be emotional as well. In the wild it would be the deer in the forest that stops moving when it hears a noise; for a child of abuse, it might be holding one's breath and staying still when an abusive parent or caregiver is near. Freeze is the response often used when fight or flight seem inaccessible due to the largeness of the threat. It can also relate to dissociation in the sense of someone becoming numb to their body and emotions. In religious trauma contexts, this can be a response used by people who feel they cannot leave their tradition or family traumatic environment and so find ways to partially "shut off" their mind and body in the abusive contexts. The trouble with this response is, as Brene Brown says in her vulnerability work, "We can't selectively numb," and so we numb what frightens us, but then the numbness can begin to infect even the good parts of life until feeling anything is difficult and being connected to body, mind, and the whole life experience is less possible.

For the survivor of traumatic experience, this reaction can be diminished by increased intention and attention to staying present in moments of safety, which can include practices interacting with the world in a very present-centered way. For persons working or living with survivors of religious trauma, it is helpful to understand their threshold for stress, sensitivities, and triggers, as well as to be able to help ground them in the present when they begin to freeze or become not present in any given moment. The worst thing you can do to someone having this stress response is to press or pressure them further into their place of discomfort. Building comfort and safety is paramount for a survivor to feel safe enough to stay present in any given moment.

The **submit/appease** response is creating no tension or conflict and moving with instead of against the aggressor or dangerous element. It is a bit like moving with the tide of the ocean rather than trying to swim against the current. As a stress response, it can be an effective way not to agitate whether the dangerous element is a person, system, or community group. This can also be a way to stay safe in an unhealthy or cult-like faith group in which being different from the crowd could isolate someone as a threat to the system, and thereby create a dangerous situation for that person. Like most stress responses, it is very effective in dangerous situations but can create a pattern of response in daily life that can lead to staying with unhealthy people or groups. It thereby makes the protection method actually a vulnerability because the person was never taught to internally or externally get out of situations that might be unhealthy or even dangerous.

When you move out of unhealthy relationships, especially religious or communal contexts, it is just more familiar. Like the devil we know, but more the devil we become accustomed to, it is difficult to leave what we know, even and sometimes especially when it is harmful. We don't mean to repeat those old traumatic patterns, but we do—we are repetitious creatures. So for survivors, it is important to be vigilant of relationships after traumatic experience, religious or otherwise. Often the support of a therapist can help filter through the information about people or people groups to help you form healthy relationships in all aspects of life. It can be hard work, especially when someone has held the protective posture of appeasing those who might hurt them, but it is possible.

Tend-and-befriend is the most recently discovered defense mechanism for someone in survival mode or trauma response. Tend-and-befriend is associated with the hormone oxytocin, which has also been called the "bonding hormone" and creates connection between humans. In the best of circumstances, it builds healthy relationships, contributes to the bond during and after birth between a mother and her child, and generally helps us connect with others. Unfortunately, like all the survival responses, it can also be turned against us in distress, or in the case of PTSD, in distress that has been frozen in place. It can lead to feelings of dependency and emotional reliance on potentially hurtful persons, environments, and community groups. Much like with the concept of Stockholm Syndrome or in the Honeymoon phase of domestic violence, a person will feel connected and emotionally bound to even the most difficult situations, persons, or people groups.

For persons with this particular survival mechanism, again like with appeasement, there may be the need for external help in identifying these patterns of affection and behavior. It is best for a person or community group engaging with someone who has the tend-and-befriend survival mechanism to help that person set boundaries, sometimes by pointing out the need for a boundary or by creating those boundaries on your side of the relationship—with love and acceptance but also a strength to keeping the set boundaries. It will help that person and the relationship in the long run.

The Many Mansions of the Heart

Teresa of Avila, the Spanish mystic after whom I was named twice, wrote a book in the 1500s titled *The Interior Castle,* which describes the mansions of the soul. She believed that the soul had many layers and each layer she described as a mansions, or rooms inside the castle of self. She also believed we entered each of these places through the doorway of suffering—something she knew well as a person who suffered extensive medical issues and pain, as well as the disappointing ache of being an activist and reformer of her monastic tradition during a time (the Crusades) when doing such a thing was a deadly endeavor. Through dying, we are reborn. Through pain, we are given access to a new doorway or mansion to the heart and soul.

The suffering we experience in trauma is initially responded to by the system described above—one of primal survivalism. If we can see it as such and begin to work to move beyond just a survival life, our pain can be a doorway to a new mansion of ourselves—a deeper space of heart, mind, and spirit. I wish suffering wasn't the doorway to depth and knowing and awakening, but it is the way we were made. It is through the death of something in us that we are reborn. It is through the pain that we have access to something that a superficial life story will never give us access to. Our heart, body, and soul have many mansions. When we move through the pain, we still wrestle with it, but we do it from this wise place—one that knows what it is like to be in primal survival and what it is like to try to survive the wilds of suffering, but one that also has been able to touch on the depths of understanding, compassion, and self beyond one individual life. When we experience trauma and pain, we join the lineage of a great many mystics, healers, wisdom teachers, and hope-bearers who found their way to wisdom through the experience of the worst of the world. This is our lineage—we can claim it, own it, and be empowered by the eternal truth that pain carries us to the deepest places where experiential wisdom is born.

There is a story of Teresa of Avila wrestling quite literally with her relationship with GodOne night she set out on mule, in the dark. She almost always traveled by mule and by night because she was without extensive funds for her revolutionary monasticism mission, and she was in constant danger by daylight—where enemies of her work might harm her. At nighttime, she's on a mule, and it is raining as she sets out on the rolling hillside of Spain to travel from her home monastery to another city where she was working to set up a new monastic community. The mule missteps, and she goes flying into the muddy, wet earth. Covered in mud, cold, wet, and seriously pissed off, she shouts into sky (paraphrasing), "Seriously?! Seriously?! All that I am doing—why? Really, why?" To which God is said to have replied, "This is how I treat my friends." With the famous sarcastic cleverness this fiery mystic is known for, she replied, "And that is why you have so few." With that she got back off the ground, on her mule, perhaps as galvanized by her anger to continue her journey as by anything else.

We can see this parable of persistence as a reminder that hurt can derail us, and difficulty can make the road we need to travel seem impossible and unending. It's stormy, muddy, and exhausting at times. But there is something sacred about the muddy places—it is the space where we prove who we are—infinite beings, capable of the impossible. You are an infinite being, capable of the impossible. Curse at the heavens; riot against the muddy road. We have to—but we don't have to stay on the ground in the muck. We are capable of the impossible—even when it seems even God him/her/themselves is on a mission to inconvenience, perturb, and injure—that is not the whole story. Hope is a relationship. Faith is a relationship. Grace is a relationship. Believe in yourself, and who knows where that belief can take you. Always remember that even in the darkest night, you are still capable of the impossible. Trauma is a muddy, rainy, sacred road. It may anger you enough to make you get up, at first, out of spite, but whatever the origin is, it is the impetus to keep riding that gets us to new places, spaces, and new mansions of our heart, mind and spirit. Scream into the sky. Rage into the rain. Do what you have to do (especially in the beginning of healing) to get back up on that mule and ride it into the next chapter of your healing.

A HEALING PRACTICE: Grounding in the Present Moment

Life in traumatic experience can feel like a tornado—wild and untethered. Part of healing from what injures us is being able to create a safe distance from the thoughts and feelings that can overwhelm a person living in traumatic experience or suffering from traumatic stress. Even the body itself can often feel overloaded—almost as if buzzing on a high frequency.

Breath, as we explored in the Introduction's contemplative practice, becomes the gateway to calming and soothing overstrained nerves and an overtaxed nervous system (which is what trauma does to the body and brain—overloads it). Once you have begun to access a slow and steady breathing pattern, as is taught in the three-part breath practice, you can begin to more wholly ground yourself—so that in the tornado-like moments you have some way to ground yourself in the present.

The following is a very simple practice, which integrates the breath of the Introduction's practice with a simple tool for grounding yourself—mind, body and spirit—in the present. Whenever you feel overwhelmed, this can be used as an extension of the breath practice to help you stay centered in the eye of the storm that is trauma and suffering, rather than be carried away. If you regularly find yourself in these moments of ungrounding, fear, panic, anger, or aggression, you can add an object as your grounding object or point of focus—maybe a smooth rock you keep in your pocket or something that carries significance to you, which you can carry without anyone else noticing. This is up to you.

1. Wherever you are, become aware of your surroundings. Where are you sitting or standing in this moment?

2. If it is possible, begin to engage with some part of your three-part breath. Even if this just means breathing in your nose and out

of your mouth, begin to engage with this practice of intentional breathing.

3. Begin to feel your surroundings. Touch whatever is closest to you—this might be the case of your cellphone, the object nearest to you, even the fabric of your clothes.

4. Notice the texture and dimensions of this object in front of you, as you continue to intentionally breathe through the moment of stress. Is the object (your clothing, phone, something nearest to you) jagged or smooth, rough or textured? Notice how it feels. If you have a grounding object, pay attention to the dimensions of that.

5. You will have memories, thoughts, and feelings flutter through your mind. You will have ideas, worries, or concerns begin to crowd your brain and tense your body. This will happen. This is part of the human struggle. Your goal is to 1) not attach to any one thought, feeling, or sensation, 2) return to breath as a way to ground in the moment, and 3) return back to the object you are using as your point of grounding.

6. Feel the breath moving through your lungs and then begin to ground your whole body in the present moment.

7. Continue to breathe and ground with your object of your choice— that which you carry with you or just something, anything, in your environment—a railing, a chair, the earth beneath your feet, a chair beneath your body. Be present with how it feels to sit; stand, and be wherever you are in that moment. Feel your feet in the ground, your body in the seat (if you are seated), and the object you carry (if you carry a grounding object with you).

8. Distractions will always come, and the intention of this practice is to return to your breath and ground you in the present moment whenever you feel carried away by the chaos of your mind, life, and body. Pay attention to the ground beneath you and your body where it stands or sits, and if you have an object to focus on, bring your attention to that object and how it feels—its weight and texture, in this moment.

CHAPTER 2

Inside the Animal

Symptoms, Jargon, and Manifestations of Religious Injury

Permanent good can never be the outcome of untruth and violence.
—MAHATMA GANDHI

I opened Chapter 1 of this book with my own story of religious wounding at the hands of a summer camp experience gone wrong. After I wrote the story, with the memory fresh in my mind, I was talking with a fellow therapist and explaining my experience.

It is not a story I keep in my back pocket; it is not my cocktail party fodder, unless, of course, it is a cocktail party rife with church-hurt survivors (and, yes, before you ask, I actually have been at many of those parties, over the years, either intentionally or accidentally).

So it was out of the ordinary that I would be telling it to a friend and colleague. It came out of a conversation in which I was trying to explain this book, what it was about, and why I was writing it.

I told her about the camp and its adventure sports premise and propaganda-schooling underbelly. I told her about the long night of bullying and my intentional movement away from church following the experience. I didn't really have a particular expectation for her response.

I knew her mother was an atheist, burned by a rigidly conservative and punitive Lutheran church upbringing, and her father was Jewish. I knew her family, and she attended a Unitarian Universalist church now, but not with any substantive regularity. I knew they celebrated Christmas and Chanukah and were put off by anything smelling of crazy-Christian. I knew her UU church back home had a gender-neutral bathroom with a picture of a man, woman, and transgendered person on the stall door.

These are the things we had discussed: our surface confluence of theology and baseline faith histories. So when I finished my story, I didn't know what she would think of my experience. She paused for a moment and then began to speak, and something absurdly cosmic and comedic happened. It was a cosmic comedy of errors, of sorts.

It turned out she had also been sent away to adventure camp, a camp that also spelled their camp with a cutesy "k" at the beginning and a long "k" name following, sounding eerily similar to my own camp's name. She had gone because friends were going and was lured in by the promising brochure pictures of kids smiling while whitewater rafting, zip-lining, and swimming. The only difference from the start was that her camp was in North Carolina and mine in Missouri.

Then she began her traumatic church-hurt story, which put my night of heaven-based- interrogation to shame. If you experience triggering from your own personal traumas with religion, you might want to skip over the next two sections detailing her experience.

She said she had been at camp a couple of weeks, and was settling in to the rhythms of the days; it seemed pretty benign, and the usual camp fare of sub-par food and crammed bunk-bed cabins.

She knew her friends she had followed to camp were Christian, and the fact that it was definitely a Christian camp became clear early on with their haphazard insertion of Jesus Christ into every activity, community gathering, and meal. Not being brought up in a traditionally "religious" home, it was a new system of functioning— not bothersome, just different.

Then one day she went to arts and crafts, and the campers were asked to make lanyard keychains for their parents. For her mother, she made a bouquet of flowers. For her father, she made a series of connected Stars of David. As she was working on her last star, her camp counselor came over and asked what she was making.

"I'm making a keychain for my dad," she said in her happy and eager 12-year-old voice. "What are those on your key chain?" the art teacher asked, pointing to her stars.

"They are Stars of David, because he is Jewish."

Nearby the ears of fellow campers and counselors perked up, as the syllabic makeup of a word unfamiliar to their ears echoed in the air. *"Your father is Jewish?!"* The shrillness of her art teacher's voice frightened her. Even though she could not register why, she knew something had just changed.

Suddenly all the counselors were huddled around her asking questions and shooting statements at her like darts at a target. "You can't make those stars in this class, don't you know that?" "Jewish! You know your daddy is going to Hell, don't you?" "Um, I, well, ok, I don't know." She stammered, nervously, not sure what to do or say.

After the art room debacle, everything changed. Word spread quickly to all the adults in camp that her father was Jewish, and soon everyone over the age of 18 on the camp grounds was approaching her throughout each day, telling her the penalties for not being Christian (earthly and cosmic) and asking her, repeatedly, to accept Jesus Christ as her personal Lord and Savior.

She was flustered and increasingly scared. She was only 12, way too young to confidently ward off that kind of harassment.

She asked her counselors to call her parents, but she had been put on phone restrictions. Word was out that she was not allowed to make or take calls. So she started writing letters daily to her parents, telling them what was happening and pleading with them to come get her.

Days passed that felt like forever. She couldn't understand why her parents weren't answering her letters, which became increasingly desperate. When she asked questions about her letters, someone, a weak link in the chain, told her all her letters sat in the camp director's office. A mandate had gone out that her letters to her parents were not to be sent.

In desperation, she wrote her grandmother, hoping maybe they wouldn't catch those letters. She was right. Her letter made it to her grandmother, who immediately called her mother and made it clear that if her mother didn't go get her, she was going to drive up to North Carolina from Florida to get her.

Her mother was in disbelief. Who in their right mind wouldn't be? What kind of camp would do that to a child?

But before her mother could react, the girl in distress got clever and began to figure out an action that might get results. She was finally beginning to understand what they wanted, and like a good captive, she gave it to them in hopes of some clemency.

Days that felt like months into this spiritual waterboarding she walked up to one of her counselors and said, "You know, I have been thinking about it, and I decided I want to accept Jesus as my personal Lord and Savior." She was greeted with a strong hug and a communal showering of praise. "Do you think I might be able to call my mom? I'd really like to tell her."

Clever girl. My friend was no dummy.

The second the counselor handed her the phone, she began feverishly dialing the numbers to her anticipated freedom. When she heard her mother's voice, she started shouting into the phone, "Mom, please come get me! Get me out of here!"

The counselor grabbed the phone away from her, and a few other camp staff began pulling her out of the room. Her counselor got on the phone and told her mother how she had been misbehaving in camp and had become out of control. They told her mother not to believe what she was saying.

Protective and insightful to the sound of fear in her own child, her mother went into a rage:

"You listen to me: My daughter is to be put in a private room, and neither you nor any of the staff at your camp are to talk to her at all! I will be retrieving my daughter immediately and will get there by morning. You keep away from her!"

The stammering counselor agreed, not that my friend's mother could hear her. But it didn't matter: Help was on its way.

A long 10 hours later, my friend's mother arrived, with a trunk full of candy (contraband at the camp) to heal my friend's wounds, and as a "screw you" to the camp staff, she began handing out bagsful to any kid with an outstretched hand. While hungry-eyed children pillaged the trunk, and my friend sat consoled and surrounded by her sisters who had come along on the rescue mission, her mother made sure all of the camp administration got a good helping of in-person yelling, replete with many a creatively strung expletive that surely made them blush.

My friend made it out, and due to her mother's emotional stamina and a good helping of both her parents' smarts, today she is a strong and determined woman, although I think it is no big leap to say the camp affirmed all of her mother's atheist beliefs and certainly helped keep her away from any structured Christianity or dedicated faith tradition to the present-day.

With a glint of cleverness in her eye, she closes the story: "I should have just gone with my Jewish friends to *their* camp. I could have made all the Stars of David I wanted, and no one would have bothered me about Hell, since we Jews don't even believe in it."

So if you read my opening story and thought, "That seems extreme. I am sure it didn't happen like that. I'm sure that kind of thing is an isolated incident," I can tell you that isn't true.

In a divine comedy kind of twist, the first person I disclosed the story to after revisiting and rewriting it, had a more extreme trauma in a near identical camp. I am fairly certain, had I begun crafting Stars of David instead of "only" questioning the heaven theology, I would have gotten the same increase in abusive treatment. As we disclosed our camps to each other, they could have been doppelgangers, twins, twisted sister-sites of fundamentalism, separated at birth.

Although in my sample size of two, my facts are anecdotal, they are some pretty convincing anecdotes. In my sample size of two, the number of people traumatized by Fundy camp is 100 percent.

As you will see throughout the book, as we explore more people. stories, and suffering, we are at the tip of an iceberg that could take down the Titanic. If in this metaphor the Titanic is Christianity and the iceberg religious traumatization, then we better have a whole lot more lifeboats. This does not mean that faith or those hurt by faith are doomed—only that we must see our weak spots, as people and as communities of people, if we wish to repair rather than destruct the boat we are in.

Lifeboats are the issue. If we carry the Titanic metaphor forward, with the iceberg as religious trauma, and the ship as Christianity, then the lifeboats would be those people in faith willing to help heal the trauma faith-based community created. Right now, as it stands, we don't have nearly enough lifeboats.

Right now we are the Titanic. Throughout this book, I will add both to the anecdotal proof that this trauma is more pervasive than you think it is, and there is already available statistical data from such sources as Pew Research Center validating that a sort of "religious exodus" is underway. Let's consider these people the metaphorical ones, who are diving off the Titanic in desperation into the ice cold waters below and specifically the Christian exodus, which shows that people are leaving Christianity (and some of the other mainline religions) at alarming rates. In science these are the kinds of statistics that require deeper inquiry.

This book is that deeper inquiry. Through the lens of trauma and with the eyes of someone who has been there, I explore the trauma of religion that is dismantling it—like a massive iceberg would slice through a seemingly "unsinkable" ship, so Christianity is being gashed at its core, and its own hubris, like the Titanic, got it here.

No ship is unsinkable.

Overview of Religious Injury

The more you understand your brain-body system and how, after traumatic experience(s) you are more prone to have your stress response stuck, the easier it is to tackle the healing process. It doesn't mean the healing process will be easy; it just means that knowledge is powerful as a first tool of healing. This way it is not a mystery why or how your brain-body reacts—it is just a matter of being a detective of your own system, its responses, and your own traumatic memory roots so you can begin to change your system's response, which changes how you experience the world.

Of course, in religious injury, church-hurt, and spiritual abuse, it is commonly a repeated or elongated process of traumatization— it may be overt traumatic experience, more subtle abuse, neglect, or demeaning behavior that builds over time. Either way, your experience and pain are valid, and there are ways to combat this inner war that plagues many people who experience trauma. This book, the stories, "life parables," and terms and practices are meant to be a primer for your healing. Your journey of healing will likely include more than this book or its practices. Healing is a communal process, and it can most definitely take a village. In my own healing journey from sexual trauma experienced in my late adolescence (the subject of my first book, *Mending Broken*) and years of PTSD, it took a number of villages. Part of my own healing process and the way it wove around my spiritual journey are discussed here, but my village included everything from yoga classes to acupuncture sessions, to contemplative practices and meditation, to writing, reading, and learning everything I could about trauma, and eventually led me on the journey to pursue helping others heal from traumatic experience.

Your journey is like your fingerprint—uniquely yours. Make your road with whatever materials and tools suit you best. I hope this text serves as a beginning to that journey—both understanding religious injury and some beginning practices for healing. The following is a list of common symptoms of traumatic stress and PTSD. You may experience some, all, or none of these if your stress response has been stuck. If you are experiencing any of the following issues or other alarming emotional or physical symptoms, see a mental health or medical provider to be assessed and begin care for these issues. You can find healing with coping tools and emotional support.

Triggers

For some, the term triggers might be well known, as it relates to mental health issues and negative experiences; for others it may be a new concept. It is generally the term for anything that instigates a memory, response, or revisiting of a past emotion or experience. In the language of mental health, this is related to something negative, which can bring on a negative response—anxiety, anger, or in its most acute presentation, even a flashback.

Examples of Triggers in Religious Trauma

In religious trauma, triggers can be certain environments like churches or chapels. They can be certain types of people like authority figures or clergy (or clerical attire). A trigger can be certain language often used in experiences or contexts of traumatic stress in religious settings (such as: saved, salvation, repentance, sin, chosen, believer/ nonbeliever, or general jargon from whatever tradition the trauma stems from, or phrases like "Jesus is my Lord and Savior," and "Hate the sin, love the sinner," or similar phrases from other traditions. It could also include certain scents like smoke or incense that remind people of religious contexts.

Simple Tools to Address Triggers in Religious Trauma

If the traumatic experience or experiences are in your recent past, the safest bet initially is usually to avoid people, places, and things that will trigger a traumatic response. When pain is still raw, it is hard to move through a trigger in a way that is not additionally traumatizing.

After time and emotional distance from the original experience, it may be possible to address the trigger when you are exposed to it by simple grounding and breathing practices to center you in your body, mind, and spirit. Many of the practices offered at the end of each chapter, namely the *three-part breath*, can offer a way to calm yourself when faced with triggering experiences.

Intrusive Thoughts and Flashbacks

When a person is triggered in some way to remember their negative or traumatic experience, this is an intrusive thought. It is a thought from an experience of the past that intrudes on a person's present life. A flashback is a more extreme response to a reminder of the past in the present. During flashbacks, people actually feel as if they are returning to a particular traumatic episode from their past. This can last a second or a minute (and longer in extreme cases), but it feels in that moment like the person is right back in that stress. The difference between intrusive thoughts and flashbacks is that with thoughts, the person is still in some way grounded in the present. With flashbacks, the person is mentally taken away and back to the traumatic incident[s].

Examples of Intrusive Thoughts and Flashbacks in Religious Trauma

In religious trauma, just like in most traumatic experiences, intrusive thoughts or flashbacks take a person back to situations of high distress because those are the thoughts most prominent in our mind—in trauma these thoughts get stuck or lodged in the forefront of our mind and this is why they are accessible so easily when triggered. This may be a specific incident of distress or emotional/physical danger, or it may just bring back the memory of a person or group or setting in which repeated trauma happened—like a faith-based space, a certain religious leader, or a family member who utilized negative dogma to abuse or diminish someone.

Simple Tools to Address Intrusive Thoughts and Flashbacks in Religious Trauma

The most effective way to deal with an intrusive thought or the emotional and physical aftereffects of it is to be able to calm yourself back down. They can be very overwhelming in all parts of the self because they engage the hormones and adrenaline responses in the body—when your brain brings you back to the traumatic place, your body and mind in the present respond as if there is danger. Our hormones speed up our body to try to get it prepared for that danger so coming out of an intrusive thought or nightmare can feel like you just jumped out of freezing water—it is a shock that puts your whole self on high alert. A *grounding practice* like the one in Chapter 2 is often the most effective way to bring a person back to the present and away from the trigger. Just creating present-centered associations as simple as, "I am sitting in this chair," or "I can feel the floor beneath my feet," can help ground you back into the present.

Nightmares

Nightmares are extensions of intrusive thoughts and flashbacks, which visit a person in their dreams. Because we have more control in our conscious minds, when we fall asleep we are much more sensitive and vulnerable to the traumatic memories, persons, or experiences. Depending on the extent, there may be a few acutely traumatic experiences (or a subconscious version of those experiences) that may show up regularly in the dream state. Sometimes, however, the nightmares are just plagued by feeling unsafe in their lives— family home, faith space, or elsewhere. So it is also possible that the nightmares will just manifest that feeling of being unsafe into dreams that have nothing to do with exact experiences someone has had, but create anxiety-based scenarios, which may seem related to no particular memory.

Examples of Nightmares in Religious Trauma

In religious trauma, like with intrusive thoughts and flashbacks, the nightmare can bring a person back to a specific incidence of abuse or negation in a person's religious experience. It can even bring into the dream specific persons who were most harmful in the person's negative experiences in religious contexts. It can also, as articulated above, manifest as feelings of lack of control, helplessness, or anxiety. These dreams might have nothing to do with specific instances but manifest in fear-based dream themes including: the feeling of falling, running from an unknown (or known) source and feeling weighted down or unable to move, being unprepared or underprepared at church or school or for a test or possibly religious ritual experience and also just generally being taunted or made fun of and feeling shame or a less-than-good-enough feeling.

Simple Tools to Address Nightmares in Religious Trauma

Often when you have a trauma-induced nightmare, the fear and even certain imprints from the dream state may leave residual effects right after waking up. That can include still seeing the figures or shapes from the dream like a shadow left over from that acute memory. A person will also often wake up sweating or with a racing pulse due to that feeling of danger, which is then translated into the dream, and back out again, based on fear in a real past-lived experience. Both *grounding* and *breath* practices are useful to center back in the present and out of the dream state. If it is a really alarming nightmare, it also can be useful to turn the lights on or get a drink of water before returning to bed. Listening to relaxing music or a relaxation CD prior to returning to sleep can also set a foundation for safety rather than fear.

Hypervigilance and Exaggerated Startle Response

Hypervigilance is really just a fancy term for exaggerated startle response. Both are terms to describe the high-alert status that the body and mind go into when they perceive danger. In normal life this would occur when there was a real crisis or feeling of danger. When the memories and feelings of traumatic experiences get lodged in our body and mind, we can be triggered to this level of hypervigilance and overalertedness when we are safe, but our body and mind believes we are in danger based on old information. Exaggerated startle response is the way the body responds to this state of high alert.

Examples of Hypervigilance and Exaggerated Startle Response in Religious Trauma

In religious trauma, as with any other traumatic experience, this kind of high alertedness can show up in our lives in the way we become oversensitive to safe things as if they were dangerous things. Being tapped on the shoulder and twitching or jumping would be an example of that, especially if the traumatic experience(s) involved some kind of bodily assault or harm. Another example would be jumping or twitching at a loud noise. Other sensitivities could be around all facets of the senses—sensitivity to touch or certain sounds, sights, smells, or tastes that trigger traumatic memories or reminders of traumatic environments.

Simple Tools to Address Hypervigilance and Exaggerated Startle Response

Because this kind of response is an overstimulation of the senses and the body based on memories stored in the body and mind, some ways to diminish the intensity of those feelings is to sensitize in new ways not associated with traumatic experience. Some examples of tools include a cotton ball or small roller of perfume or natural oils contrary to the triggering memory. A common one I use is lavender because it is soothing to many people, but you could use a favorite scent of any kind. Another example is to carry a token or reminder of something positive or grounding with you—this could be some silly putty, a rock from the beach, or a silver dollar. Anything that is weighty enough to hold in your hand but discrete enough you can keep in your pocket will work—that way you can hold it when you need to ground without anyone even seeing it.

Anxiety and Panic Attacks

Anxiety is a natural response to a literal danger or threat but in traumatic stress it gets thrown into hyperdrive and can exceed what is necessary for self-protection in certain situations. In its most extreme form, it can induce panic attacks where the brain-body cannot regulate the level of distress being experienced and the system essentially overloads. It overloads to such an extent that often people who are having panic attacks sincerely believe they are having a heart attack—the symptomology can be almost identical. A person's chest feels acute pain, their muscles contract, their throat can constrict, their palms sweat, and their pulse races. In some cases it can lead to hyperventilation—which is when the breath speeds up so quickly it can make you dizzy.

Examples of Anxiety and Panic Attacks in Religious Trauma

In religious trauma, anxiety is rooted in the original spaces and places that induced traumatic response—this could be due to physical or sexual dangers, but it also can be from a general feeling of invalidation by persons or a faith community group based on identity or differences from the system/community. Being a woman, gay, a person of color, or even disabled could be a reason someone was made to feel less than in a particular community, and that sense of invalidation can lead to anxiety not just in that group but in entering other spaces—there is a constant fear that this new place or space might offer the same painful invalidation. This makes it hard to build intimacy, try new things, or enter new spaces. When this fear becomes acute—due to injury in previous faith environment—just entering a new life experience or environment can lead to a pre-emptive feeling of fear that can become incapacitating.

Simple Tools to Address Anxiety and Panic Attacks in Religious Trauma

Just breathe. As simple as that sounds, regulating breath is the first and greatest antidote to panic. When we panic, our breath gets held or sped up to hyperventilation level. I teach every client, contemplative practice student, and grad social work student breath-regulating practices as a baseline for everything else we work on in their respective contexts. Breath is life—and regulating breath is the first step to regaining life. Breathe again. Breathe fully. Explore practices that help you breathe fully and completely. The three-part breath is a starter practice in this book, but expand from there. Just steer clear of any breathing techniques that have you hold or speed up your breath—in trauma healing there is no need for any more of that breathing in your life or your healing practices. Down the road, if you want to use those you can—but not in the healing process.

Anger/Angry Outbursts

Anger is the external cousin of anxiety. While on the face of it, people whose traumatic response presents as anxiety and anger may seem on other planes, but they are really just two primary ways that our brain-body system tries to ward off danger—as we discussed in the traumatic response concepts. Also, anger can present outwardly or inwardly—anger presented outwardly is seen as rage and even violence; anger directly inwardly is emotional or even physical masochism and self-hate (the cousin of guilt). They are equally destructive.

Examples of Anger/Anger Outbursts in Religious Trauma

In religious trauma anger can be a healthy response, or it can bend toward an emotionally destructive compulsion. It can be empowerment and empowering; it can be justice and justice-seeking, but it can just as easily be destroying you inside as you are telling yourself it is empowering and justice seeking. True empowerment that lasts and justice seeking that has stamina needs to burn away the rage to get to the good stuff—you need to eventually let go of hate to do the best for yourself and others in this world. Anger can destroy us. In the healing process from religious injury, like in the grieving process, there is a season for anger and there are moments when it is necessary and righteous. Eventually you will have to give up the habit of rage "against the machine" (aka religion) to transform yourself into more than just opposition to what you loathe. Our best selves are the promotion of what we love. This is no easy task—to burn out the hate—but it is an essential part of healing. Just like religion is not, in and of itself, the answer to all healing, rage against religion is not the final answer to healing. When anger is consuming your thoughts, actions, and much of your time for the person, persons, or religious system that hurt you—that is when it is no longer functional and borderline compulsive. We are addictive creatures—and hate is especially addictive. Rage gives us adrenaline and cortisol—that is why we have the term "adrenaline junkie." I have seen it hundreds of times—where the rage post-trauma consumes everything good in a person, client, or friend, until nothing is left of life but that anger. This is toxic in religion as in all other injuries. It is hard to understand, but it is essential for healing. Be more than your anger—use it to help you heal and motivate you, but then let it go. It is the only way to be fully whole again. Religion and church can not be everything for anyone—either in the trenches of it, or in opposition to it. We must move beyond the absolutes to become healed and whole again.

Simple Tools to Address Anger/Anger Outbursts in Religious Trauma

Since anger is anxiety's cousin, the same basic rule applies—breathe again. Breathe slowly and deeply. This will give you enough time to think about your thoughts, words, and actions before you act from anger. You cannot take back what you have already done—but taking a few breaths before choosing to act is the first step to learning how to change your course and make calm decisions. Especially with the speed of our culture and action and response times between texting, tweeting, Instagramming, and beyond—sometimes stopping to take a breath is a good thing for all of us.

Complicated Grief and Loss

Grief and loss will enter into every life, but when we are hurt or hurt others, the grief can feel like a tsunami of pain—too much to bear. Like complex trauma, complex grief is not just one incident, but a web of pain and loss. In religious injury, this pain is very complex. Depending on whether a person is in the community that hurt them or has left that community, the loss can include the loss of family, community, and faith tradition. Even when the place and people who raised us hurt us, to lose all those things when a person walks away is extremely painful. That is a deep layer of grief. Then if the trauma includes some version of negation of the self—based on gender, race, sexuality, or even personality—it can create a huge amount of grief, which can border on shame. Even when we want to believe the truth about ourselves—that our life is valuable, and we are good and enough as we are—years of being told the opposite takes its toll. A loss of the person we might have been, without that level of hurt, negation, or abuse, is a great loss and needs to be validated as true grief. There is a large amount of grief and loss in religious trauma. Validate yourself and all you have lost. Give yourself time to feel those wounds and then, when ready, prepare to address the grief so it doesn't take you down.

Examples of Complicated Grief and Loss in Religious Trauma

The details about how grief and loss can manifest in a complex way after religious trauma begin in the definition, however, it cannot be understated how much grief there can be for being told you are less than valuable as you are. If you are a woman, gay, or a person of color in a faith tradition that marginalizes those aspects of yourself, you probably have felt that pain. It is doubly painful and disappointing when it is family inside the faith community who mirrors that invalidation and when you are told the source of your "not enough" nature comes from the ultimate "parent" such as a God figure. It can take time to feel valid as a person again, but the loss of that time of life you felt less-than could remain. Beyond being traumatic this experience of invalidation, suffering, and pain can manifest into complicated grief—grief that goes deeper and lasts longer than normative grief, which we work through and are able to move onward from. Complicated grief like trauma that turns to PTSD requires its own healing—we have to mourn what was when exiting unhealthy belief systems. This loss is often loss of family, friends and a God image and each one has to be grieved in its own way and its own time.

Simple Tools to Address Complicated Grief and Loss in Religious Trauma

I find ritual and ceremony to be deeply powerful ways to address grief and loss. Because the pain can be so deeply felt and complex, it can be beneficial to seek a therapist or support professional to help you move through this process and the ceremonies for release, which can help you move beyond the pain. That said, there are a number of practices offered in this text that can help begin this process. Letter writing to a former version of yourself whom you feel is lost is one ritual. Burning your pain in a fire ceremony or using a letting-go ritual with water is another way. Anything that engages us with natural elements or cultural traditions can offer great tools to release grief.

Trust and Intimacy Issues

It is no wonder that after experiencing abuse or being diminished or bullied within an unhealthy faith structure or community, it is hard to trust and build intimacy. This is both communal and interpersonal. Since a community is made up of individual people, and the people who hurt you in faith community are also often friends and family, it is very hard to rebuild a foundation of trust. Then if the traumatic experience(s) or belief systems created negative feelings or shame/guilt related to who you are as a person in relationship to others, and so often as a sexual being, entering into relationships after that experience can make one feel very conflicted. Even when we know what we learned about ourselves is not true, it is hard to uproot the triggers to shame and guilt for loving someone, being intimate, or having a positive relationship to your own body. Additionally, to build trust if the foundational relationships of your early life (family, faith, friends, God) were all abusive or negative, a person has to learn trust from the basement up. This is no small feat.

Examples of Trust and Intimacy Issues in Religious Trauma

Trust and intimacy, as well as the underlying understanding of love and being loved, are rooted in how we are taught those elements by family and our community systems in childhood. Since many people's religious trauma begins inside of those early systems—the family and the family in context to the religious community—the ability to have a healthy model of love is very difficult. In unhealthy religion, love, God's love, the community's love, and even the family's love is contingent on playing by a set of rules—it doesn't mirror an omniscient love that can be found in healthy religious systems, but rather presents that all love is conditional. This makes love and trust a very fragile element—conditional on doing all the right things the right way; otherwise love can be taken away and acceptance rescinded. This fragility sets up a very delicate and breakable capacity for trust and an incapacity for deep intimacy—which is born out of being who we are authentically and being loved for our authentic self.

Simple Tools to Address Trust and Intimacy Issues in Religious Trauma

Learning love and self-acceptance, and the requisite trust and intimacy that build out of that, must often be learned from the ground up after religious trauma. Begin with practices that make you feel good about yourself or hobbies that help you connect with who you are and what you love. Once you have a foundation of self-esteem, self-acceptance, and practice accessing your true self (not the self that anyone else wants you to be), you can begin to find external love, trust, and intimacy with less fear. It is a slow process, so begin small. Find one thing you love and dive into that, with all you are and all that you can be. Then you can manifest your own safe space from which to build up love.

Isolation and Avoidance

When you feel you aren't, can't be, or aren't allowed to be your true self in your community or family system, removing yourself as much as possible from others can seem like a temporary solution to a more permanent issue. When a person leaves their religiously wounding community, that response of withdrawal from the world can be hard to break. Also, if you are struggling with knowing who you are and are fearful, based on past experience of sharing that with others, removing yourself from the world may be lonely, but it can also feel safe. If your self-esteem has been broken down, it can be hard to imagine that other people want you in their life and world. Isolation is a common coping mechanism post-trauma to avoid triggers and more hurtful experiences, and as a method of keeping away from old people, places, and things from the past. This response over time, however, can feed depression, low self-worth, and create even more complex issues of guilt, shame and trust.

Examples of Isolation and Avoidance in Religious Trauma

Sometimes this can be selective isolation post-religious injury and woundedness—the most likely example would be avoiding any faith community and any program or even conversation that includes religious words. When it begins to invade all manner of life is when it can become emotionally dangerous—we need people and companionship. It becomes more problematic if you don't have even one person or place where you feel safe. This is why starting small to build back trust is valuable—it removes some of the barriers and wards off isolation that can grow to near agoraphobia in some cases. I have worked with many clients who began with fear and anxiety, and then moved to selective isolation, and then to a place where all interaction felt unsafe. Like anything else, being around others is something we practice each day by investing in something or someone. With the Internet, we have the advantage of interacting with others at a distance. That said, real life interaction is as important, arguably more important, in this age of one-click relationships.

Simple Tools to Address Isolation and Avoidance in Religious Trauma

It can be understandable after being hurt by your religious community that withdrawing from life and the world seems like a viable and reasonable response. In some ways it really is, but it can also create a habit of avoidance that can become as hard to break as any other symptom or traumatic response. Sometimes people will return to some kind of community group or tradition—we are social creatures, and without some human interaction life is difficult; also without some community of meaning or shared values it can also be difficult. Often something people miss the most when they leave their tradition was the community element, as well as shared experience and views. Even if in the end that wasn't true, there is a conflict about the lack of loneliness in a religious context. Engaging in some new friendships and eventually even community groups can heal this dimension of trauma. It can be as slow as it needs to be—but we are social creatures. Many people over time return to some faith, religious context, or philosophical/shared values community. Whether it is a meditation gathering, a yoga satsang (community meal), political party network, professional network, or even some different facet or sect of one's faith of origin, being connected in life is a healthy component of a life fully lived. Testing yourself with one relationship or picking one community group to engage with—even the most benign like softball or knitting—is a good way to learn to be in community in some way again without the unhealthy components.

Guilt and Shame

Nearly every Catholic joke ever been written begins with some line about guilt and religion. As a side note, although I was plenty hurt by people and elements of my Catholic upbringing, I actually didn't have an overwhelming amount of shame. I view these as just an irony to articulate that every person's story is different, but often religious hurt can include some nature of guilt and shame. Also, if someone in a religious context abuses, one often sees the rules or doctrine of the tradition used by abusers to validate their abuse and maintain silence and secrecy around their crimes. Guilt and shame can become imbedded in a person like a tattoo of pain, which is difficult and painful to remove. Issues of gender, sexual orientation, and sexuality are dimensions highly laden with guilt in many unhealthy traditions and doctrines. This can often take time to work through and shake off, layer by layer.

Examples of Guilt and Shame in Religious Trauma

Guilt and shame in religious trauma can be built in early in life— which impacts the ability to feel good enough or valuable before a person can even understand guilt or shame. Being who you are—a woman, a gay person, a person of color—and being negated by your community can be very painful—especially when it is woven into how you understand yourself in context to your family, your belief system, and God. Shame is difficult to shake off when a person is told that the origin of shame and the one that validates the need to be ashamed is God. How do you even begin to untangle that belief structure? It is not easy.

Simple Tools to Address Guilt and Shame in Religious Trauma

Building self-worth is a huge component of addressing guilt and shame, as well as being involved in conversations and communities who validate you for who and how you are in your most authentic self. For some people, this could include getting involved in justice or advocacy volunteer work in the area of their own negation. The important thing is to keep in a mind frame of empowerment rather than rage in these contexts. Advocating for and having a voice in issues about a part of yourself that was once seen as "wrong" by your faith community can be empowering, but it also can feed rage. You just have to be careful. Find ways to empower your true self—and spend your time around those who validate who you are. Slowly the pain and shame imposed by the outside source—a system and/or family/community—will begin to melt away as you realize you have value and worth.

Emotional Numbing and Dissociation

When we have been battered and bruised, sometimes the only or most accessible recourse is to shut down. In the mildest form of this, it can be as simple as tuning out what is being said or where you are in any particular moment—this is something all of us have done. In response to a greater sense of danger, manifesting the freeze trauma response becomes more acute and numbness can become more pervasive. The primary coping mechanism for those who have experienced trauma and couldn't physically leave their circumstances may have been to numb out. This can mean shutting down feelings, but it can also involve completely removing oneself from the situation. When mind and spirit exit an experience entirely, it is called dissociation. Dissociation can be the floating above yourself and seeing what is happening experience, often experienced by those who have survived sexual trauma or extensive physical abuse. It also can manifest as losing time due to being completely absent or blacking out during an experience (not due to substances but just the brain exiting the situation as a stress response). If dissociation is more severe, mental health treatment should be sought immediately because this process can be a danger to daily life and functioning.

Examples of Emotional Numbing and Dissociation in Religious Trauma

Depending on the type of trauma experienced in a religious context, the nature and intensity of the emotional numbing and dissociation will vary from person to person. Acute physical and sexual abuse can lead to more dissociative states to self-protect—primarily because being able to leave might not have been an option in the initial trauma, and so the brain created this escape hatch to protect you from having to be present for the experience. If the pain and suffering wasn't as physically as emotionally dangerous (which all trauma is), then being able to numb to feeling states—fear, anxiety, anger, etc.—is often how someone deals with being or staying in a religiously hurtful community. As we know, we can't selectively numb or dissociate, so often this way of coping will carry over to postfaith-hurt experiences and be harder to manage once the brain is in the habit of exiting discomfort.

Simple Tools to Address Emotional Numbing and Dissociation in Religious Trauma

Grounding, mindfulness, and guided relaxation practices can help teach the brain and body to stay present and focused in peaceful moments so it can access those resources also in distress. For more severe dissociation, therapy with a trained trauma therapist is necessary to learn ways to contain stress and find safe space in the mind, body, and physical world. Once the brain-body system can integrate a sense of safety, it will begin staying present rather than exiting when stressed.

LIFE PARABLES: Triggers

The below "life parables" are extracts of stories of persons interviewed about their experience of religious injury and spiritual trauma. Some are the real names, and others have been changed to protect those who don't yet feel safe to speak out. The following Life Parables describe these people's experience of triggers, those negative and sometimes visceral reminders of their traumatic religious experiences, and how they impact them when these experience them today. The content of these stories are intact, although some language has been slightly altered for readability and flow.

DAVE: Some organized religions and their environments, like churches, still trigger me when I see or go inside them. Even traditions with which I don't have a history, like the Episcopal Church, can trigger me with the ritual of kneeling or taking communion or singling a hymn I sung as a kid. It can bring me back to the absolute ideologies I learned from each of my family members, in different and dysfunctional ways, that one way of belief is right and all others are wrong. This was so conflicting when, after my parents' divorce, each part of my family played tug of war for me, my time, and my beliefs. When I was with my dad, I had to be Catholic. When I was with my mom, I had to be Methodist, and when I was with my grandmother, I had to be Southern Baptist. It was so confusing to me, and I ended up feeling like if everyone thought their way was right, then there was probably no right way at all. So even today the sight or rituals of institutional religions remind me of that painful tug of war of family and faith.

BILL: I think a lot of the canned answers that church tries to offer still trigger me, especially blaming people who don't want to come to church as if they are less devout or too lazy or whatever. The idea that people care less because they aren't sitting in church pews on Sundays (where I would see very faithless people sitting week after week) are somehow less good or valuable to God is a huge angering thing—one of my greatest religious triggers. Also related to that trigger for me, as someone who sits inside a faith community, is when leadership or membership of church spend time asserting there is something wrong with people who don't want to come to church. This always seems more like avoidance of looking inward to see how they are contributing to that, how they have been uninviting, or how they are or aren't living out faith in their own lives.

Additionally, as a person of color, to hear white men in church talking about their issues and difficulties with political correctness (expressing how they are inconvenienced by it) is very hurtful and triggering for me as someone who has been hurt by people of faith before, and as a person who has been marginalized in church communities because of my racial background. My sisters and brothers of color don't want to be insulted publically, and with mostly white denominations and diocese, I have experienced the lack of understanding and empathy for people of color—in talking about and even toward them when they show up in the pews. For me, that is a very hard pill to swallow.

MARG: I am very triggered any time I am in a group of anti-gay Christians (whether five or 5000); it impacts me to such a great extent it causes me to experience panic symptoms. Nobody even has to say anything. This panic trigger also occurs when I am around those who use the anti-gay smoke screen that states "Love the sinner, hate the sin." I feel right through their words into an inherent feeling of danger. I also have to be very careful to limit my exposure to anti-gay Christians' remarks overheard in person or on TV, or to anti-gay writing. Even moderate exposure causes me to get emotionally overloaded and unable to control my feelings of anxiety, panic, and fear.

KISHA: When I enter Pentecostal churches I am triggered. I hate seeing the elevated pulpit that congregants have to sit below and look "up" at. I believe the subliminal psychology in doing that causes congregants to subconsciously worship and/or deify the people who sit in those elevated seats. I can even be triggered when I see these churches' services and content about their worship on Facebook. I am also triggered and angered when I encounter church people and they ask me where I attend church as though they assume I *have to* go to church somewhere. In order to protect myself from such triggers, I usually try to avoid those situations altogether. However, during those times when they are unavoidable, I generally talk them over with my therapist and/or with friends.

FAY: Writing this, joining PTCS (Posttraumatic Church Syndrome) group on Facebook, and counseling (as a therapy provider) others with similar stories are all triggers. I find that I can use this, at least in my profession, because being aware of my own weaknesses and pain is so important when being a therapist.

DEB: Certain phrases will trigger me, such as "I was depressed and I gave it to God and now I am healed." I'm sorry, you may have gone through a period of depression, but when you are diagnosed with depression, generalized anxiety disorder, and have been through the process of ruling out PTSD (I still self-medicate too much to get that diagnosis I guess), it's not as easy as just giving it up to God. We need medical intervention just like anyone who has a visible ailment, and I feel when people use those kinds of phrases they minimize pain, suffering, and the healing process. Another phrase that really triggers me is, "God wants us to have riches, those who are still poor are stuck in the mentality of poverty, and you must not have enough faith to still be in that position". This makes me think, "Spare me". My grandparents were piss poor and had the most faith of anyone I knew. Normally when I get triggered in these ways. I react with anger (by venting to the trusted people), because I can't believe this kind of stuff comes out of their mouths. I also try to keep in mind that they may mean well but are terribly misinformed.

ANGIE: When people fill their vocabulary with God, blessed, Jesus, etc., it really triggers me. Going to church is a trigger for my nightmares. And the phrase "God told me to [fill in the blank]," makes me want to choke the people saying it..

DEANNA: Purity culture is a big trigger for me. The moment someone suggests that young women need to show less skin so their husbands can stay righteous makes me go into a rage that blares through my temples and makes me want to get drunk and take my clothes off in front of anyone who will look. The pervasive and persistent attitude that my body is not my own, and that just my moving through life is somehow dirty and tempting to someone else, reopens many wounds. When someone says the spiritual but not religious are just wishy-washy people who can't commit and are afraid of admitting they are sinners demonstrates to me that they are tone-deaf and blind to the spiritual temperature of this world. It hurts. I am also triggered when someone says something completely ignorant toward members of other religions. For me, it demonstrates they don't care (even though the church claims to love everyone) and they don't believe that God cares, which is so untrue.

MELINDA: Words that trigger me are: forgiveness, reconciliation, femininity, Evangelical. It still upsets me when people say things like: "We are persecuted as Christians here in America. We are at war!" The debate about homosexuals and whether they can worship in the church also triggers me. I am also triggered by the idea that the only way to be a Christian is to be part of a church.

EMMA: My sister and I learned we were safe with the Native Church as Native American women and the people there brought safety and comfort, but if you were not within the Native Church (church on a reservation with Native American people), you were not safe and not accepted. For years I was triggered walking into a non-Native church, because after leaving the Reservation the White churches were the places where we were most alienated, ostracized, and meant to feel both other and less than anyone else. It was a very lonely feeling—to go from feeling God and comfort in church on the Reservation to feeling so unsafe and unloved by how we were treated in White Church. For years after being emotionally hurt and threatened by members of the White church (and also our community when we lived off the Reservation), I was unable to walk into any church at all—it was just too painful, scary, and triggering of my religious wounds at the hands of those in our first non-Native (White) Church.

REFLECTION ON LIFE PARABLES:

While the trigger examples offered by Dave, Bill, Marg, Kisha, Fay, Deb, Angie, Deanna, Melinda, and Emma are spread across a wide spectrum, they all define the ways they felt negated, less than, betrayed, alienated, and ostracized by their faith communities. Beyond that, they also describe how the code of their hurts was written across their lives in the form of triggers (things about the faith tradition or any faith that bring back the memory and hurt of their experiences)— which they have to encounter and address, always taking them back to the origin place of their hurt. We should all pay attention to this roadmap of hurt—it helps us learn about ourselves, others, and the power of institutional and communal hurt on someone, long after the original pain experience has long since passed.

Triggers can have a longstanding ripple effect in the life of a person. Both as the persons who might be triggered in religious contexts and those in religious contexts trying to understand the wounded, it is important to understand that it takes time to see, address, and diminish the impact of hurtful triggers in life. If you are experiencing religious triggers, then understand that it is reasonable to feel triggered in religious contexts if your wounds come from religious sources. With time and work, you can begin to release the hold they have on you. For those who are trying to understand persons triggered by religious ideologies, languages, places, and spaces, you have to understand the weight of this hurt. You can't diminish or shame them into changing—if you try to do that you will just repeat the abusive behavior that caused the triggering in the first place. Love, patience, and complete acceptance, with time, can begin to help those suffering these triggers release the pain for themselves and in relationship to others.

The Redemption of Symptoms: Putting the Brain-Body to Work

The value of the brain, body, and trauma symptoms is that the change of them into distress proves one truism—the brain and the body can change. So if this is true, then there is a reciprocal truth—it can change again. The most absurd hope and reality of posttraumatic stress and its infiltration so completely into the body, mind, and spirit is that the infection of pain can be reversed. In traumatic stress, and the reverberations of response in the fibers of our being, we are taught that whatever the nature of the brain, body, and spirit, it can be changed. Powerfully, painfully, excruciatingly, the system of our selves can change. What this proves—with the most rudimentary understanding of science as I know it—is that Newton's law applies everywhere. Every action, in the universe, has an equal and opposite reaction. For every suffering that is imposed on us, and the symptoms that take up root in our veins, there is the potential (maybe even a mandate) for an equal and opposite reaction. The force that binds us in suffering also offers us a bastion of hope—that we can and are capable of an equal and opposite response to that traumatic force. We can change. Brain science and the study of the brain proves this is true with each new study of the brain. It is not easy or mandatory. It is only possible. We can reach into that possibility at any time. If the safety of symptomology, or the triggers of trauma and response, are not something you are ready to let go of, that is ok. Those trigger responses have served you well. They protect you from the pain, but they also keep you cornered off from joy. You can change, but you can do it only when you are ready. I don't want to push you into that space. If you have experienced religious injury and spiritual abuse, you have been pushed enough for a lifetime. You can heal. I offer you that hope. I also offer you the option to say, "Not today." When you are ready, the tools are here. Community is here to welcome and embrace you into the space of the possible—even when it seems impossible. You decide if or when you want to enter through the garden gate of hope—that choice is yours.

A HEALING PRACTICE:
Creating a Safe Space/Guided Visualization

When we experience trauma, especially in the places meant to be safe—faith and/or family—it can make it hard to feel safe anywhere else. The safe space visualization allows you to create an internal safe space, one of your own making, which you can carry with you everywhere and all the time. This safe space becomes what we call in therapy a "transitional object"—think Linus's blanket from Charlie Brown. A transitional object is something we can carry with us that brings a feeling of safety into our lives—the hope is that over time, like poor Linus was meant to do (if he hadn't stayed an eternal child), we create a sense of safety that doesn't require the transitional object. The visualization is a version of a transitional object, as described in some of the tips to deal with stress. You may want to carry a physical object that reminds you to calm down and find that internal safe space—like a coin, rock, or something small enough but with enough heft to hold onto. The physical object can remind you to use your breath or access our internal safe space when you need it. Over time, you can work toward not needing the physical or visual object as much—and being able to feel the inward-oriented safety in life as a whole.

1. Begin with finding a safe and quiet place to practice the safe space visualization. Get comfortable—whether that is seated in the chair, on the floor, or lying down.
2. Close your eyes, or if that isn't comfortable, find a fixed point on the ground to look at that won't bring any outside distractions in on your practice.
3. Begin with your slow and steady breath to slow you down and ground you. Focus on your slow and steady breathing as long as you need to until you feel ready to move to the next phase of this practice.
4. Imagine a safe place—if you have a reference point of a real place in your life where once you felt safe, go there if it is comfortable. If you don't have any real safe place in your memory, imagine a place you have always wanted to go or your ideal environment— for some that might be a beach, for others, the mountains. For some it might be inside and others in nature. Find your selected space and visualize it.
5. As you visualize your safe space location begin to look around— notice the environment. What are the sounds, scents, and sights in that space? Add objects or elements into the environment that remind you of safety—maybe the warmth of a fire, the sound of birds singing, or the feeling of sitting on a cozy blanket. Whatever makes the space safer and more comfortable, add those elements into your safe place.
6. Take your time becoming familiar with your safe space—until everything about the space is vivid in your mind. Remember that

in this space you are safe and that you can always return to this place whenever you need it.

7. Return to your safe space daily if you can—before bed is ideal as it brings positive imagination into your creative brain before sleep, when trauma can work its way into your subconscious. Using this practice before bed is like building a healthy internal environment that can combat the negative feelings, thoughts, and nightmares that can come in sleep for those with trauma or unresolved stress.

CHAPTER 3

Through the Looking Glass

Religious Injury and Traumatic Stress

*In the end these things matter most: How well did you love?
How fully did you live? How deeply did you let go?* —Buddha

I tend to use a lot of *Alice in Wonderland* metaphors when I speak about trauma and healing. My husband would probably prefer I used far more *Matrix* concepts—and if that suits you we can go that direction, too. Both Alice and Neo struggled to live in the world as it was, each seeking something greater than the sum of their parts, each coming to a crossroads where they had to choose a potion or a pill to move out of the world as they saw it and into a new reality—one in which everything turned upside down, but somehow truth became far more authentic. In many ways, that is the journey to navigate through suffering—it comes down to the choice to see or not. We can live in the world we have been offered, unexplained, unexamined, or we can choose to go deeper and see all the scary things, but also more acutely, all that is beautiful about reality.

As a very small child I used to look at the world as it was and searched for any way to make it more acute, painful or joyful. I just wanted life to be more profound. I would sit in my room or classroom, or at a play-date, and create stories that moved beyond my reality into something I thought would be greater. I was always a dreamer. The learned lessons of life and the irony of life helped me see that I didn't need to create a super-reality to experience things acutely. Actually I learned that my hypersensitivity to the world—blessing and curse that it was—would bring me all the acute joy and pain that any one human life could handle.

It came in tidal waves and tsunamis, sometimes with excruciating pain and occasionally with excruciating joy, far more powerful and immense than anything my daydreams about superheroes and castles could have ever imagined. I always thought life would never be enough, and along the way, I learned that much of it often felt like too much.

Ravaged by identity tectonics in adolescence, a Latina adoptee, born in the Andes, and raised in Jersey suburbia, only an express train away from Manhattan, not quite sure who I was by anyone's standards, I remember a feeling of being so alone in a sea of activity. Later adolescence brought sexual trauma, with two assaults by different perpetrators, and the grand mountainous landscape of PTSD to navigate for the better part of a decade—ignoring, facing, fighting, and healing through the years. Then, when the altitude of that suffering subsided, I found myself without a country—someone who didn't know where she came from or where she was going (infertile from endometriosis and unable to get pregnant), plagued again by the "who am I's" that I thought I had left behind. Moving through that tsunami of hurt, I found myself a year later, hurdling into the onset of fibromyalgia pain and sudden asthma—painful and breathless, acutely alive.

I was Alice. I was Neo. I had taken the elixir of true and excruciating life and gotten everything I asked for—each pain surmounting the one before it, both rolling tides and high-reaching mountains of pain. What I learned from that experience is 1) Whatever our expectations of life, we are given much more than we could ever imagine—good, bad, and ugly, 2) Life will always surprise us—painfully and beautifully, often in equal measure, 3) We don't need to create grand machinations and adventures—life is the greatest and most terrible adventure, without any need for expanding on the script, and 4) We can see what is, take what is given, and grow it into something greater than the sum of its parts.

We need to look at life through the looking glass and see what is first. After that we can be liberated from the cage of what we have been given to make it what we want it to be. This is the way we rescript the journey—this is the sacred trail. Initially, however, we must see the pain for what it is—we have to know our dragons, mad hatters, white rabbits, and Agent Smiths, before we can battle them adeptly and surmount them. We can surmount them—but first we must see them. That is why Neo has to take the pill to see the world as it is— then, and only then, can he battle the evil in his story.

Deeper In: Many Faces of Trauma

To understand trauma we have to see where it lives, how it manifests, and the many ways we can describe the traumatic experience. Sadly, we are in a human universe in which there will probably be only more, not fewer, permutations of traumatic experience moving forward. The benefit of all these terms is that they validate the human experience of pain and illustrate that different pains, even different traumas, manifest slightly different in the human experience. Childhood trauma is going to have distinct impacts on a person, as is the repeated experience of trauma throughout the lifetime. It can help us identify markers for different traumatic experiences and the uniqueness of the intergenerational or historical traumatic experience and how these might be distinguished from an injury to the moral self. We now can see how living with a person who has experienced trauma or working with trauma survivors regularly can traumatize people.

The field of traumatology (study of trauma and practice of treating trauma) is also beginning to isolate different issues specific to someone who has experienced trauma in a religious community setting. The latter is in the infancy stage of both exploration and treatment. The clinical world is only on the precipice of religious injury, or what I am calling "sacred wounds" study and practice. Sadly, the need only seems to be increasing exponentially by the day, as more stories come out about this kind of traumatic experience. In this chapter, we will explore some of the above listed traumatic issues and what traumatic experience looks like in religious contexts, and review some examples of this hurt experience.

Developmental Trauma

While developmental trauma is not an official diagnosis in the Diagnostic Statistical Manual (DSM), it has become a commonly used term to define trauma experienced by a person while still in the developmental stage of life (infancy until the early 20s). What science has been able to illustrate about the developing brain is that it is much more malleable than in later stages of life. Therefore, trauma experienced before the brain is fully developed impacts not just the emotional and psychological state of a person but the actual structure of the brain. As we will discuss in the next chapter, religious and spiritual trauma is often experienced beginning in childhood and, as such, it has to be looked at not as just emotionally detrimental but also as something that might have impacted the way a person thinks.

Complex Trauma

Complex trauma is traumatic experience beyond a single incident of traumatic experience. This kind of trauma is experienced repeatedly over an elongated period of time and has most often been attributed to situations of domestic violence, childhood sexual or physical abuse, and combat trauma. It also can be a compounding of trauma over the life cycle—the revictimization of someone who might have been abused in childhood and then abused or violated in other ways throughout the lifetime. Often when a person has a traumatic experience that is emotionally unresolved, there is a greater tendency to be abused or violated again; this is known as re-victimization. Throughout this book, we will explore the nature of complex trauma as a common dimension of religious trauma due to how it impacts a length of life, often childhood (thereby also being an issue of developmental trauma), and can often be a precursor to trauma throughout the life cycle. Part of the intention of this book is to provide a way to look at the religious traumatic experience as a means of resolving the pain, suffering, and (in many cases) PTSD experienced by people who have suffered this wound in silence.

Intergenerational Trauma

Intergenerational trauma is traumatic experience that spans beyond the lifetime of one single person and impacts generations of people. Part of the difficulty of intergenerational trauma follows the logic of the old adage: Those who cannot remember the past are doomed to repeat it. In this kind of trauma, the pain, hurt, and suffering have become so ingrained in not just a person but a family (perhaps even a community) that it can become invisible, woven into the fabric of the way things are, and as such not visible enough to address. Common examples of intergenerational trauma might be multiple generations of combat veterans with PTSD, a family of abuse whose parentage and grandparentage includes the same abuse, a family with historic issues of addiction, or suffering generations of marginalized people such as Native families living on an impoverished reservation. In the case of religious trauma, there are many hurtful belief systems, doctrines, and mores, which negatively impact people for many generations. Issues of shame or latent anger then become ingrained in the family or community system. Additionally, if the abuse or marginalization of a gender or sexuality is prominent in a faith culture, then there can be generations of those who are being hurt or abused by the same system all living together and reflecting issues of self-hate or other-hate into the next generation.

Secondary Traumatic Stress/Traumatization and Compassion Fatigue

Secondary stress is the traumatic stress experienced by persons who sit with the traumatic pain of others, which can include both professionals in the helping field but also those who are the loved ones of trauma survivors. Similarly compassion fatigue is the emotional, psychological, and spiritual exhaustion of someone who sits with people through their pain. In a religious system, this could be people who are working with a community and the survivors of abuse within that community. There have been experiences where people who have been called into the center of a religious community's abuse scandal end up holding much of the pain and, in extreme scenarios, can even manifest the symptoms of PTSD themselves. Other ways secondary stress can be experienced is in the intergenerational trauma situation where family is experiencing the residual effects of a family member's trauma; it also can be experienced in the support system of a person experiencing trauma and PTSD. In religious trauma, this can be family members who are not part of the hurting system, spouses or romantic partners, or friends. It is important in the process of any traumatic experience to validate the power of this secondary stress. It is as powerful and real as that of the primary traumatized person and must be addressed with love and kindness, as it requires its own healing.

Moral Injury/Spiritual Injury

Fairly new, but powerfully important, to the trauma lexicon is the term *moral injury* and the extension of which can be considered spiritual injury. This means any experience that impacts a person's morality or spiritual value set. This was originally considered to be something a person perpetrated on another that negatively impacted or went against their morality system—this was commonly found in those who had to do things in a combat zone that would go against their moral system on the home front. As the concept and its treatment has grown, it has been extended to include anything that might negatively impact someone's morality, whether perpetrated against or by that person. In the case of religious hurt, this concept takes on an even deeper meaning that, as of yet, does not seem to have been explored. In the case of religion, the morality of the system might, at some point of wounding or fragmentation, go against the inner morality or intuition of the individual. This is a very complex and confusing experience for someone—when what feels wrong in their intuition and heart might contrast with what is said to be "right" by the system at large. This is the crux of what makes it so difficult for a person to leave their religious structure or system—it means going against the morality system of one's upbringing for a personal morality structure. Needless to say, this takes an immense amount of courage, and it is often near impossible for people who have imbedded the system of their upbringing into their adulthood.

Sacred wounds don't fit into a technical set of terms, but rather a lexicon that I have created to discuss the wounds that touch the personal moral center, the heart and the soul, and the emotional experience of a person. This includes what is defined above, found in a religious system or context. The sacredness of these wounds has a dual meaning—they are wounds in the sacred places of the self (the mind, the body, and the spirit), but they are also sacred in and of themselves. They hurt the most sacred parts of us, but in the healing place, we are able to find powerful personal transformation—and that is sacred, too.

The Breadth of Religious Trauma

While there is no way to illuminate every corner of religious wounds and trauma or depict every scenario of church-hurt or spiritual injury, I want to offer a few examples of what it can look like.

This is not an exhaustive list, but it is a reference point for those who have experienced what feels like trauma in religious contexts or those who might be seeking to better understand this kind of traumatic experience. Again, this is a primer and is a limited list of the many permutations of hurt in faith spaces.

The following are some common examples of people's experiences representing trauma inside religious institutions:

- A person who has been physically or sexually assaulted by a religious figure, leader, or community member OR whose physical/sexual assault or abuse has been co-opted by a faith leader or institution or deemed as "ok" by doctrine (God's Law).
- A person who has been abused by family or friends within a faith/ religious culture or institution and has been shamed or guilted into believing it was his or her fault due to church doctrine or distorted faith text references—and had those references or the abuse reinforced as "ok" by anyone else in the family/faith system.
- A person who has been deemed "lesser than" due to their race, ethnicity, or gender based on a religious doctrine, text, or faith group's history of marginalization of that or any people group.
- A person who has been told he or she is wrong, sinful, or going to hell because of who they are due to their sexual orientation.
- A woman who has been forced into a variety of kinds of submission to a man in ways that she is not comfortable with or in ways harmful to her spiritual, physical, emotional, or psychological health.
- A person who was shamed or called sinful for asking questions within a faith culture or tradition and told that questioning anything from the group/institution/religion is a sign of sinfulness or weak faith.
- A person who has been ridiculed, bullied, or threatened for any reason by a religious or faith institution—especially for questioning or leaving that group/community.
- A person who was excommunicated from a faith group/religion for disagreeing with practices of that community, its leaders, or its members.
- Anyone who has ever been made to feel he or she doesn't belong, or is less than or sinful, or unworthy, based on nothing more than being who he or she is are or communicating feelings.

Trauma Refined by the Living of It

Part of this book is dedicated to the voices—the brave, the gentle, the angry, and the meek. Being able to tell your story is a deeply healing experience. I know, as both someone who has told my story of hurt as well as read many others on my journey of healing, that we need to both tell and hear stories. We are anthropological creatures— we want to excavate the truth everywhere it exists, and we get chills when we hear truth relayed to us, especially the bold and painful truths of pain and healing.

To honor this truth wherever it resides, I collected over a dozen stories from people who have lived through a variety of church-hurts and religious wounds and were willing to speak them out loud. They are also spread across the spectrum of healing—some are still in the deeply hurting place, and others have moved through their pain and found light. Each part of this process is valuable, and each story should be told. As we explore the experience of religious trauma and healing in this book, I will share pieces of these stories along the way—the vivid and living lamplight of what is true.

As a wise teacher of mine once said—what is true here is true everywhere. This is true of these stories and truths. What is true here *is* true everywhere. Pain is sacred, and in the stories of pain and healing in this book, you find what is true everywhere. Listen close and find reverence. For those of you suffering religious wounds, I hope it brings you solace and some comfort. For those of you who are seeking to understand this kind of wound, I hope it will punctuate your learning in a powerful way.

LIFE PARABLES: An Introduction to Church-Hurt

BILL: I was part of an emerging community in Colorado with some post-evangelical folks trying to sort out what happened to them growing up. We were in this post-Christian culture where we were all just trying to figure it out; one of the key words was relationship and community. I saw so much dysfunction around that. A lot of people in the community had been burnt by megachurch and Church celebrities. But in our small community celebrity was more insidious when it began to form around a microcelebrity, one person in the community who had weight and gravitas. There were different factions in our small faith family aligning with different personalities and different microcelebrities. Each of these faction-heads had very different views and takes on faith, God and the community, and it all became very dysfunctional.

The community was free flowing, which meant no hierarchy, but also no oversight. There was no accountability, but rather, personality cults. I realized for me (and I affirm not being with institutional church), I need an institution that can have oversight, so that if someone is screwing up, it can be addressed. Of course, with each community of faith there are light/shadow sides and I, personally appreciate the structure and accountability when things get chaotic. There are emerging expressions of church that can be healthy, but that was not my experience in my Emerging Church community. It felt like people without a story trying to make one. They weren't informed by tradition or church in general, but at the same time, they were informed by the ideas from their painful church pasts that they found wrong or hurtful, and it felt like they wanted to recreate the whole thing from the ground up.

That is incredibly draining, and there can be so many blind spots. It was total confusion for me because I couldn't process how different the reality was compared to the intention for that community. In some ways it was more dysfunctional than the Southern Baptist culture I grew up in. In some ways I am still processing what the hell happened. With the lack of tradition to sustain us, it was a whole structure built on personalities. There were people hurt by faith who build the community, and so many of them came in with conflicting and untrustworthy thoughts about people and faith, which manifested as hurting other people. In some ways it was even more hurtful than splitting and differences over doctrine because we all came in with an expectation of living deep in a safe community, each coming out of hurting faith, and then this new community ended up hurting people more.

By saying it was safe from the hurt of church past, then replicating hurt in a very intimate way, it ended up betraying people at a deep soul level. The whole community ended up turning on itself and self-destructing as a result. All of it was extremely disappointing and hurtful for me. Creating this emerging expression of church was supposed to be about not being like institutional church, which we all felt had spit us up like a cog in a big wheel, and then we did the same thing all over again.

FAY: I married an abusive man who was bipolar. At 18 I did not see the signs, and neither did anyone else who knew him before our marriage. I spent 15 years in an abusive relationship, and then he left, deserted. We had two small children at that time. This is when the church left me the first time. At that time I did not recognize how traditional my upbringing had been, but I found out. You should not divorce and definitely never remarry. Women should be submissive to their husbands and do everything they could to keep them happy. So I was left, single and alone forever, or so the church said.

DAVE: My aunt killed herself in 1997, when I was 10 years old. She was a drug addict and a nurse and got fired for stealing drugs; she lay down on the train tracks. I heard someone at the funeral giving "condolences," saying that she was going to burn in hell for all eternity. She was the sweetest person in the entire world. What kind of God would do that? Was it was the belief of everyone who was there that she would suffer forever and ever? When I heard that, I remembered someone telling me once that every second you experience on earth is like a million years of pain in one moment in hell. How terrible is that for someone you love?

I always believed in God 110 percent, but for a long time I felt as if he would pick on me. Growing up with a terminal illness (cystic fibrosis), I remember thinking it isn't fair that God did this to me and not everyone else. When there was abuse going on in the home, again I would think, "Where is God now? Why would a loving God allow this to happen to me?" It is a hard thing for a kid to comprehend. I would say my wounds didn't actually happen in one establishment. It was the culmination of different sects of religion telling me different people were bad. Catholicism and Southern Baptists said, "Our way is the way, and other traditions are wrong." Whenever I was with one family member or the other, I felt like I had to be the right kind of person for their tradition (my grandmother-Baptist, my mother-Methodist, my father-Catholic). It felt like different religions pulling me apart.

REFLECTION ON LIFE PARABLES

It is important to understand that religious trauma can be experienced in a variety of contexts, shades, and levels. For some, the spaces that are refuge (emerging/organic progressive communities) might be a place of hurting for others. For others, it might be rejection of any kind found in faith spaces, which people enter assuming absolute acceptance—this is a great hurt that is both community based, but also related to an understanding of God or the divine. Sometimes it is about absolute laws that don't reflect love, but just law for law's sake—which make people believe that if law is greater than love in religion, then religion has no value. It is important to understand the wide scope of pain and suffering in faith spaces and be willing to hear people's stories to fully understand their pain. We must listen to the stories of the wounded with absolute love if we ever expect to be in honest relationship with them. As people hurt by faith, which looks like rejection, diminishment, or law, it is hard to believe in anything again. That is totally understandable. That said, hope, grace, and love are whatever you make them—and you can believe, despite those that show an unloving version of faith. There is hope even despite all the human foibles standing in the way of the best representation of God, so often in life.

HEALING PRACTICES

Depending on where you are in your own hurt and healing process, you can select one or all of these exercises to take part in. For some it may be too soon or too painful to use all of these tools, but they are here and accessible when you are ready. The great thing about a book is that you can always turn back the pages to a practice you passed over or use a tool again to gauge where you are in a new place, stage, and phase of healing.

Writing and Creative Expression Practice

PART ONE: On a scale of 1 to 10, measure the depth of your sacred wounds or spiritual pain in your life at present and the status of your relationship to your faith of origin. If you don't know how to calculate this kind of pain, imagine the scoring system this way:

1. *You feel slightly distracted throughout the day by whatever issue is plaguing you, but you can still focus on daily life.* You are still imbedded in the community group or relationships with people who might have hurt you. Perhaps the hurt isn't that acute at present.
2. *You think about this issue throughout the day and week.* You find yourself thinking multiple times a week about specific scenarios that hurt you .

3. *You find it more difficult to spend great lengths of time with the faith community/person(s) who have hurt you.* It is harder to let things go when you disagree with them.

4. *You are beginning to find increasing differences between how you feel or think about the world and the worldview of your faith community and its members.* It is harder to let things go that inherently feel "wrong" to you—even though your feelings contradict the larger doctrine of your religious group. This is very confusing and part of you feels sadness and anger, but there is also a part of you that feels conflicted and shameful for disagreeing with the larger group and doctrines.

5. *You are beginning to isolate from people, places, or things that remind you of your hurt or the community/people/persons who have hurt you.* You feel slightly lost and not sure where to go or what to do next—in relation to your hurt or in general. You spend a lot of time questioning others but also yourself—as if you are weighing the scales of what is right and not sure where you'll land.

6. *You are beginning to read books, connect with people or groups on the Internet, and actively seek insight out of your primary faith group.* Most likely you are doing it anonymously or with a pseudonym because there is a lingering fear that people in your faith group might find out what you are doing. You disagree with a lot of what happens, is said, and/or the doctrine of your faith group, but you don't feel in a position to leave it. It is very anxiety inducing and exhausting to feel as if you are sitting between two worlds, but it feels like there would be too much to undo to even think about leaving.

7. *You may have spoken up or asked a question of your faith community or its leader(s), and the response was suspicious or condescending.* You are beginning to feel depressed or enraged at the idea that you might have to spend the rest of your life in this system but not quite sure you want to leave. You begin to think about what and who you might lose if you walked away from your faith community. You feel like a stranger in your own life but not sure where else you would go if you left.

8. *You might begin to test the boundaries with close family and friends, creating "for instance" examples to see how they might respond if you left your faith group and/or began to speak about the ways in which*

you have been hurt outside your faith group. Your exploration is expanding in the world outside your faith community—both virtually and possibly in person at some other local community group.

9. *You are beginning to feel the flicker of someone inside yourself that is more than just what you have been taught.* You feel a little bit of freedom internally but also a lot of fear. To deconstruct everything you have ever known feels like it could be liberating but also terrifying. Some might call this moment an existential crisis of sorts. You are questioning your meaning, faith's meaning, religion's and spirituality's meaning, and what you are meant to do with your life—and where you are meant to do it. It is a very confusing time.

10. *You may have completely removed yourself from the faith community where your sacred wound experience(s) occurred and are considering what your next life move might be in a different direction.* You are feeling the loss and grief that someone might feel at the death of a loved one. It feels overwhelming. There is a part, however, that might feel exhilarating—like you are finally able to be the truest version of you, or at least the beginnings of that person.

11. This practice allows you to see where you might be in your process of hurt or healing. While the above scale is a stage system, it is not a hierarchy—to be in stage 1 or 10 at any given point or time is equally valid. Some people are hurt by religion and stay, and others leave. Some stay and feel unhappy; some stay and find balance for themselves. Some leave and feel unhappy; some leave and find balance for themselves. Wherever you are in this 1-10 spectrum, there is no wrong place. You are where you can be, and that is ok. The scale is only a way to see yourself and others in a compassionate way. The definitions are loose and are just examples—you might define 1-10 differently for yourself. Feel free to recreate the spectrum as it works for you or relates to your experience.

PART TWO: Once you have selected your number on the scale at present and/or created a spectrum of your own that suits and defines your own journey, find some way to express where you are in your journey of hurt or healing. You can do this by writing a short story, painting a picture, taking a photo, writing a poem, or building a sculpture. Create something—and interpret "create" in whatever way suits you. Create something from your pain so that even in the difficult spaces you can always have something of beauty to reference, and remember your pain as both deconstruction *and* creation. Make something that means something to you.

Contemplative Practice

You may feel overwhelmed by your own process of hurt and healing, whether you are continuing in or outside of a religious or faith community. It can be exhausting and painful—sometimes it feels like it is too much to take. Sometimes it can feel very lonely. Use the following practice on days you feel overwhelmed—just to clear your head, heart, and spirit space. We all need stamina for our spiritual journey. This is one way to create space and build stamina for the long road. Sometimes moving forward is also about periods of letting go.

Thought Release Visualization-Clouds:

1. Find a safe and comfortable place to do this practice. You can be sitting in a chair, on the floor, or lying down—whatever is most comfortable for you.
2. Close your eyes or keep them lightly open and focused on a point on the ground that is not distracting.
3. Imagine a bright blue sky across the landscape of your mind, dotted with white clouds. Imagine that each and every cloud represents a single thought in your mind.
4. Begin your slow and steady breath—imagine your breath as a gentle breeze, moving the clouds across the blue skyline.
5. If you feel crowded by the thought clouds, you can move them farther back on the horizon—so they are smaller and farther away from you. This can help with detaching your emotions from your thoughts.
6. Remember: Your thoughts are not you at your deepest and truest self. Your feelings are not you at your deepest and truest self. Say this over in your mind as much as you need to, to help you detach from your thoughts and the associated feelings.
7. Watch the clouds as they move across your mind, carried by the gentle breeze of your breath, one thought at a time. Observe the

thought as it passes. Watch it without judgment or criticism, and without blame of self or others.

8. Let each thought pass one at a time, carried by the gentle breeze across the landscape of your mind.

9. Whenever you feel overwhelmed with thoughts and feelings, you can close your eyes and watch those thoughts until the process becomes slower and less chaotic. If you can't close your eyes, look up to the sky and observe the physical clouds and practice thought watching using that natural landscape.

Continue this practice regularly. Build up to 10 minutes of practice at a time. You can then build beyond 10 minutes up to 20 minutes. The ultimate goal of most meditative or mindful practices is to reach a maximum of about 20 minutes. Don't let this frighten you—in the beginning it may be 1 minute or 5 minutes, but keep working on it. It will decrease stress and increase your ability to have control over your thoughts and your mind.

CHAPTER 4

Faith of Origin

Religious Roots and Family Issues

All the trials we endure cannot be compared to these interior battles.
—TERESA OF AVILA

As an international adoptee, born in Colombia, I spent the better part of my childhood and adolescence imagining my origins. This ranged from imagining my birthmother trekking down from a mountain tribe to bring me to the orphanage, run by Grey Order nuns (that part is true), before she trekked back up to her community, to envisioning a secret affair between my birthmother, a maid, in the home of Pablo Escobar, who had to take her love child to the orphanage in the covert cover of night, before my birthfather, kingpin of the South Americas, even knew I existed. I share this embarrassing bit of false childhood narrative only to describe the ways we try to make sense of our origins—whether familial or faithful.

After finding out I couldn't have children, I wondered where I began or ended if the genealogy of "me" was a one-woman family tree—more like a genealogical stump. I wasn't sure what to do with being a genealogical stump. I had no beginnings or endings—literally speaking. I never thought it mattered until it was a fact. Then it was all that mattered.

In the depths of my personal existentialism, or as Anne of Green Gables might say, "depths of despair," I was hit by a reminder by way of an eccentric feminism professor who was an equally eccentric clairvoyant, and my namesake, Teresa of Avila. Let me explain—in brief.

At the very end of my sad attempt at babymaking, I found myself in a kind of desperation—the kind that no longer had anything to do with the source intention (to create life) and everything to do with the forceful perseverance of the truly stubborn. It became entirely about doing the undoable, and by doing so, being able to create or recreate my entire life story, only the smallest of delusions for this once-dreamer of the impossible. Somehow I had entangled my lack of identity found in my adolescence with this need to have some genetic future. For someone who had lived a life and experienced a childhood built out of family of choice rather than genetics, I seemed to have lost my compass entirely.

I became obsessed with my origins and depressed by my lack of future—in the literal sense. Then Teresa came back into my life. About a decade earlier, a feminist professor of mine had insisted I read *Interior Castle* by Teresa of Avila. Teresa happened to be my namesake—first brought into my life, as far as I knew it, in my naming by the Grey Order nuns a few decades earlier when they realized I was born on October 15, her saint's day. I forgot about her for a couple of decades until urged to read her manifesto in undergraduate school by my slightly odd feminism professor who fashioned herself a bit of a psychic. As psychic as she wasn't, in this one way she read exactly what I needed, possibly by serendipity far beyond her capacity.

So Teresa came into my scope again when I found myself unable to manifest life in the way we girls are taught we are intrinsically created to do from the first story of "where babies come from." Then I went to this clairvoyant session with a circle of women, hoping for one last hope, that some psychic electricity would ordain me for biological parenthood—when all biology spoke to the contrary. Whoever she was and whatever her true talents were I don't know, but she told me one thing, which carried with me from that day forward. I asked to speak to my mother, and she asked which one, an odd question for a universe that never presupposes adoption as a person's life story. I said my birth mother. The message that came was this, "We are manifesters. The both of us. We burn bright and hot, and together we would have been a disaster. Whatever way you are meant to in this world you are a manifester."

What is truth and what is fiction? I don't know. But I know the message I received that night was true, and I realized it was outside of biology. There are many ways we manifest. I remembered in that moment my namesake, Teresa of Avila. She never gave birth to a single life, but she gave birth over and over again in her lifetime. She was a manifester, and she was my primogenitor. Out of that moment and a few subsequent encounters with that Teresa of my origin since, I realized that she was my birthplace. She was where I came from—in a way that was truer than biology and more real than time. The limitations of my small scope of view didn't diminish the expanse of my lineage. I realized that I was born of mystic fire—and everything else was semantics. Long before I would have used the word "mystic" to describe the fire within that always burned, I had a birth mother. I had always had a birth mother. Her name was Teresa.

I only explain this to illustrate the way we box ourselves in by the stories we tell ourselves of who we are, the life we lived, and the meaning of it all. When we look outside the limits of what is, we see what is possible, and the fire of that reality is greater than facts, history, or biology. We are all meant to be something more.

We have to learn that our life stories, our life scripts, are what we make them. We are given the raw and literal material of life—we have to see the roots of our origins—but then we have the latitude to manifest our truths in whatever way liberates us from them. We see our truth and then create our destiny—this is the intrinsic story of healing.

Let us begin with the roots. Since we have to see the origins of our familial and spiritual stumps, or trees or vines, before we can rescript our futures, we will begin with what is and from that we will mold the clay into what is possible.

Faith and Family Systems

We learn everything from our primary caregivers. How does a person know what love is, what it looks like, or how to love another person? They learn it because their primary caregivers teach them about love and how to love. In therapy, the term for the system that raises us is called our "family of origin." The family that raises us is our family of origin, and they also become the place of origin for everything we know, believe, and feel. They set the template for a life of understanding the world. The potency of this early life is the reason why trauma experienced in childhood is so devastating and damaging.

This is made even more complex when we look at trauma occurring within the family system that is also surrounded or enmeshed with a faith system. In my study of religious community systems and trauma, I have come to call this system that encircles the family system as the "faith of origin." The faith of origin is the religious system that has "raised" you, for all intents and purposes. It is the system that (usually) surrounds the family system and enforces or reinforces the values taught by the family. When both family and faith systems are healthy, they reflect to a child a value system that can facilitate caring and kindness, love for all others, generosity and graciousness, and a sense of accountability to do good to others. When either system does not reflect those values, it can be powerfully hurtful. Imagine if the family system is abusive, violent, or unhealthy, but the faith system is healthy—there is confusion for children between what they are being taught in the pews or faith community versus what happens behind closed doors. This can lead to becoming jaded about one or both systems. Conversely, the family system could project and enforce a healthy kind of love but the faith system, community, or leadership could reflect something different. This also can lead to jaded impressions of at least the faith system.

The most hazardous and common kind of interaction between the family of origin and the faith of origin systems that breed faith wounding is where the two work together to enforce and then reinforce a negating God image. If we think of the parent figure in a house as the ultimate figurehead of right and wrong, then we can think of the image of God as the ultimate form of parentage. If we consider abuse, rejection, or shaming by a parent as the most damaging traumatic wound (or at least the one with the most extensive impact on a person throughout their lifetime), then imagine how much that is compounded when the "parent" is God. Imagine as well if the family, community, and religious institution creates and then reinforces whatever abuse, rejection, or shaming a person is experiencing— and then tells the traumatized person that God brought his or her suffering on and that it is deserved. Talk about some family baggage. This is cosmically bound family baggage.

This is also why it is so difficult for people to see their way out of this kind of God and these kinds of systems. If my family is the place of my abuse/hurt, but my faith community is a place of refuge, then

I have some way to reflect goodness into my life and onto myself. If my faith community is the place of my abuse/hurt, but my family is a place of refuge, then I also have some way to reflect goodness into my life and onto myself. If my faith community and my family reflect only the abuse/hurt and mutually reinforce it, unless I have some other frame of reference (which is less likely in environments where family and faith community are so linked because they are often very insular as well), I see myself *only* as they see me. I have no frame of reference to tell me I am good or should not be ashamed, or that God or the world can love me exactly as I am. There is no one to tell me it is not ok to be hurt or abused by people or systems when everyone I know is part of a shaming or abusing system. This is what makes religious trauma so insidious and difficult for people to get away from or find a voice to say, "No."

When I meet people in my study of religious trauma, I begin with this question, "What did the God of your childhood look and act like?" How people answer this is often the greatest reflection of how they see themselves and the best definition of what kind of faith community they come from. If it is healthy, loving, and nurturing, then the God of their childhood will reflect that—and in a healthy family system their parents will look the same. In an abusive system and family, the lack of love and acceptance will be reflected and the God-father will often look much like the home-father. God is personified and father is deified in the worst and best scenarios according to the love or abuse of that family/faith system.

At this point it is useful to introduce a few more terms. These terms are therapeutic terms, which offer ways to look at unhealthy relationships. If we consider that either family and faith institutions can be independently or jointly unhealthy systems, it is important to understand unhealthy relationship concepts as well.

Understanding Family Issues

Codependency

Codependency is a relationship built on an unhealthy amount of neediness—where one side is the inherent caretaker, and the other is dependent on the caretaker to function. Neither is fully or wholly independent of the other; it is like being born with two arms and two legs but living as if you only have one of each—thereby making half your limbs weak to the point of immobilization. With addiction disorders, codependency is due to the compulsive nature of the need and the common instance of one or more people in a codependent relationship being addicted to drugs/alcohol. In an unhealthy or abusive religious context, codependency can be rampant. Community members are codependent on the institution and the dogma, the institution is dependent on the doctrines, and the abused/traumatized persons often find themselves in the middle of a web of codependency—on the family system, community, institution, doctrines, and beyond. This is another reason leaving an unhealthy faith community can be so hard—it can feel as if leaving a very dependent relationship and years of only using half of your spiritual and emotional limbs can leave someone very weak when he or she decides to leave. It takes time and work to make those limbs function again, but it is not impossible. Understanding the inherent dependency in the unhealthy faith relationship is a valuable tool for beginning to repair the damage.

Enmeshed/Enmeshment

Enmeshment is a function of codependency. To be enmeshed is as it sounds. It is when two things are strongly bound together, like a wire fence. Each strand of one is tightly wound around the other, so that all parts of one overlap with the other. When someone is enmeshed, it is hard to identify personal feelings, thoughts, and aspirations—this person is so wound around someone else or another community/system that it is impossible to know the "I" outside of the "we." Unhealthy religious and family systems rely on enmeshment to keep people bound and wound tightly around the center. If I don't know where I end, how can I know what I want or need? If I don't know what is you and what is me, how will I ever know I can say "no" when something seems wrong? Like the overarching tent of codependency, it is important to acknowledge enmeshment in your life to begin untangling yourself from the wires around which you are bound. It is very hard to become unwound from enmeshed religious and family systems that fall inside of enmeshed religious contexts.

(Family of) Addiction

You may remember the adage from Karl Marx: "Religion is the opium of the people." While we can say this is a bit oversimplified and jaded of Mr. Marx, it is hard to deny there is a certain tenor of addiction to unhealthy religious systems. The most detrimental religious systems are often the most seductive in their fundamentalism. Fundamentalism gets a bad rap for good reason, but it makes life so simple. Everything is clear—black and white—and carries with it no room for opinion. While for some of us that may seem horrifying, for people who have felt lost inside their own life choices or have grown up in a system of fundamentalism, independence can seem terrifying. This is the bread and butter of fundamentalism—to prey on the fear of ambiguity and to promise a sense of peace and ease with their (whoever *they* are) brand of certitude. This kind of simplicity can be addictive. I have seen the way it feeds people's need to feel safe in a way that is undeniably alluring, alluring in a way, like Marx articulated, that could be synonymous with an opiate. For years I have counseled people in recovery from unhealthy religious systems and substance addiction. Both are very hard to kick, and relapse can happen.

Unhealthy Attachment

Attachment describes what the root word implies—how we attach to one another. Namely, in psychology, it specifically describes how we attach to other people from our initial experience of relationship with our parentage, and then is translated or imprinted onto every relationship afterward. The way we attach can be healthy or unhealthy and conditional on that primary relationship (parentage in family and faith) that teaches us all we know of love and loving. In a healthy attachment, we know we are loved, but we are not so dependent on what we love that we feel we can't function without it/them. In a healthy attachment we can know how to love and be loved, but we can also be independent beings.. In an unhealthy attachment we are overly dependent on our love object (be it person or deity) and feel we cannot function without being in their presence constantly or having their assistance to do even the basic functions of life. Unhealthy attachment is the sweet spot of a fundamentalist system—it feeds on that need and holds on too tight. Learning to find the balance of love, community, and faith is a learned experience, and it can be very difficult to move from unhealthy to healthy attachment—it means restructuring the whole way a person functions in all manner of relationship. Like anything else, it is possible. With work and time, all of the dysfunctional learned patterns can be changed, and knowledge begins that process.

Where Church-Hurt and Religious Wounds Begin

If we go back to the early years of life, we can see the template for everything that follows. Specifically as it relates to religious wounds, what we learn about life and love from family and faith will inform how we see ourselves and the rest of the world.

The following are a few examples of how the God and father/parent figurehead showed up in the lives of people who experienced childhood (and often continuing into adulthood) religious trauma. These are based on interviews in which these people were asked a specific question (see below) about their childhood experience of God and church. Each had articulated experiencing religious trauma and church-hurt and participated in a survey I sent out to collect data on this experience of family of origin and faith of origin wounding.

LIFE PARABLES: Childhood Images of God

DEB: As far as I can remember, God was to be feared, and he was constantly judging you. Jesus was my uncle who dressed up every Easter as Jesus and re-enacted the story of his crucifixion and resurrection. (He was one of the few light-skinned members of the church and had blue eyes. I wondered many times if that was the only reason they chose him.) I didn't have much of a concept of Jesus as our Savior, or being a part of the Trinity. I just remembered he was the best character in the book. I don't believe we were taught about Heaven as much as we were about going to Hell if you are a sinner. I remember watching movies with beheadings as a young child, and I pretty much concluded that was my future. I went to mostly Pentecostal and Baptist churches growing up, and we were taught that Catholics and Jehovah's witnesses were Satan worshipers. Oh... and that God favored men over women.

MELINDA: When I was a child, our family went to the local, somewhat large, Presbyterian Church. But my Grandmother was charismatic and took me to various charismatic meetings when I was old enough. When I was very young, I believed that without saying the sinner's prayer, asking Jesus into my heart, I would go to hell. I was terrified of the darkness and loneliness of hell. I very much wanted to please God and be found worthy. I was sure, as a small child, that I was a sinner in need of God's love. But, frankly, this was highly influenced by my physically punishing Dad and emotionally absent Mom. As a child, when I pictured Jesus, He was in the clouds, or surrounded by children. But looking back, the concept of him being an adult man whom I was supposed to love seems a little creepy.

KATE: I grew up in an Irish Catholic family. My mother is all Irish – the youngest daughter in a family with 22 children, all having the same father. Her mother married her father at age 19, after his first wife died and left him with six kids. My grandmother went on to have 16 children of her own. My mom had eight kids, and I was the fourth born and the first daughter.

I say all this to give you some orientation about the circumstances of my early life, but we weren't a stereotypical big, happy family. We were poor, and my parents were overwhelmed and unable to properly care for us. My mother worked full time (in the 50s, this made her unusual) because she had no choice, and she was an alcoholic for about half the time I was growing up.

We went to Mass every Sunday, made our first communions at age six, went to confession every other Saturday, got confirmed at age 12, and went to Catholic schools whenever they let us in for free. Despite all of this, I don't have a single memory of taking the idea of God seriously. It might have to do with being brought to a church where the officiants faced away from the congregation and spoke in Latin, or with the complete absence of girls and women at the altar, or with the rote nature of the Mass itself.

It might just be that I saw no evidence in the faces of the people around me that what was taking place was supposed to have meaning. Everyone seemed tired, bored, and waiting for it to be over, and that's what I was doing, too—for 18 years.

HOPE: Childhood faith in God was pretty passionate and intense. I loved and wanted to please Him, but I also had a strange relationship with Him due to my home being deeply religious and grounded in faith, yet abusive in many ways. As I grew older, my views about God became complex and confused, and yet I always still desired and sought a relationship with Him. I longed passionately for His comfort, and once as a preteen, having cried out to Him one night, "God, I wish I could just feel you hug me!!!" I experienced very distinctly what felt to be a hug. That helped me to hang on. As I matured, I could look back and see that I developed kind of a push-pull relationship with God—desiring Him and His involvement in my life, yet feeling walls and barriers due to the impact of the abuse. I don't remember clear images in my mind about God, Jesus, or Heaven beyond the pictures in storybooks .

DAVID: God looked exactly like my father. I still see an old man sitting on a throne in the clouds. I just don't fight it any more. I associated God with father. My dad was a strong disciplinarian, and I saw God as strict. Jesus was more like a buddy, so that is how I maintained my spiritual life—through Jesus—but being obedient to God at the same time. It was as if I was afraid of "father" and didn't want to make him mad, so I was very obedient but inwardly screaming.

REFLECTION ON LIFE PARABLES

From these five stories, a few themes emerge in terms of the God-parent/father who shows up in many of the early religious experiences of those persons wounded by faith. First, God is a man, an angry man/ He is an angry, misogynistic man who appears (specifically in Melinda's account) somewhat like a real-life abusive father figure. Second, this God talks an awful lot about sin and hell. He is selling fire and brimstone, and this is understandably terrifying to a child. It's a bit like a belief system built on Grimm's fairy tales, but much more frightening.

To be fully transparent, this isn't the account of every interviewee. There is not an angry God in other's people's childhoods, which you will read about later in this book. If we remember that what we learn in childhood is expressed throughout our lives, it is understandable that for people like Deb, Kate, Hope, Melinda, and David, it is going to be harder to avoid being abused by people/entities who look like their original parent and God figure.

The primary task of this chapter is to set the foundation for where religious trauma can, and often does, begin. It is also to offer insight in where the angry God complex begins in family and religious upbringing and review how damaging that can be in early childhood. This chapter is about looking at faith and God through the lens of your own childhood to see what your faith of origin looked like. Maybe it was healthy and nurturing, maybe it was aggressive and abusive, and possibly it falls between the two places. The important thing is to see what your origin story looks like and to understand those who have been abused by religious communities and leadership through the lens of their origins.

Although it can be even more difficult, we sometimes need to look at the religious abusers through the lens of their family of origin and faith of origin belief structures. At the heart of most evil done, outside of truly inborn sociopathy, is someone who was told they weren't good enough by people or some image of God. Not that we don't ask for justice for evil done, but it can help us to understand that even those who do evil have often also been wounded at some point, or been taught to hurt or hate as part of their own faith and/ or family of origin. It is rare that I have found an abuser in a religious context (again, outside of a sociopath—someone who is incapable of any human emotion) who wasn't in some way invalidated or abused by their parentage—whether earthly or their image of God-parent. This is not permission or even absolution for the kinds of heinous crimes perpetrated by those who abuse—as a survivor of trauma I know how hard that forgiveness is to give—but it may help just to understand the "becoming" process of abuse and abusers as well as those who have been abused.

If you take nothing else from this chapter, take a moment to look at your own life and those in your midst by the measurement of from whence they (and you) came—starting with the self and working outward. We can learn a lot about our present by looking at our origin. It doesn't need to take forever, just long enough to see the trajectory of our life based on our beginning. Then we move forward. Then we can learn how to change what we want to have the life we are capable of, not just the one we have been given.

The Cosmic and Human Parentage: Double the Parentage and the Hurt

I hate it when people say, "There are no atheists in foxholes." I dislike it because it feels like a capricious and oversimplified appropriation of the wartime experience for the purposes of a catchy evangelism slogan—like the kind you would find on an overly gaudy billboard along a major highway. Also, as therapist for the Department of Veteran Affairs and working with hundreds of veterans for nearly a decade, I think it is a horribly misguided slogan. My reply (sometimes just to myself in the pithiness of my own brain) when someone asserts this statement is often, "There may be no atheists in foxholes (which of course there are), but there are a hell of a lot of atheists exiting foxholes."

War taught me, in a way no other experience has before or since, the ability to stand up to most of the difficult questions of faith, life, and suffering. This is not to say that religion or spirituality in and of itself couldn't withstand this line of questioning—but very little of deep spirituality makes it off of the assembly line floor for mainstream religion these days. That material that comes prepackaged to our doors makes it very hard for a person going through real suffering to believe in the other side of hurt. Even more complicated, when the hurt or the wound is created in the place where the faith system is being sold, it becomes nearly impossible to believe in anything. Much of what passes for religion these days is, like for so many veterans I have worked with returning from war, creating atheists; limping and fractured, crawling out of the wreckage of their suffering and into the world.

The reason the contemporary branding of faith cannot hold up to the scrutiny of suffering is a multifaceted problem. For many people I have treated (both out of literal war or the war of being wounded in and out of faith spaces) over the years, the religion they were offered was one in which, simply put, good things happen to good people and bad things happen to bad people. If I take all the doctrine, dogma, and education most people receive over the first third of their lifetime (which, sadly, for some is the extent of the teaching they receive) and summarize it—that is usually what people I encounter universally say. Since the world does nothing if not disprove this credo at every turn, it is no wonder people become jaded or disenfranchised with faith. If the hurt and traumatic experience is from a religious institution, its leadership, or its membership who said, "Follow our rules, and you will be safe. Follow our rules, and you will be saved," then people find themselves doubly hurt when they find out this is not true. The first betrayal is they were given a false worldview, and the very person(s) who violated that worldview were in the same system selling that story.

Does this mean there is no such thing as complex and dimensional spirituality? Of course not. Sadly, however, it is not the faith most people have grown up with and inside.

Childhood Faith and Life Development

As children, we are developmentally meant to begin life with a concrete understanding of the world. This is why it is no wonder that many children's early imagery of God, facilitated by the nature of icons and storytelling, is very concrete and related to the world they live in. This is why so many children's early visions of God is a white man with a white beard and a long flowing robe—this is the God-image children have largely been fed, and it is very visual, tangible, and easy for a developing child's brain to grasp. As articulated earlier in this chapter, for some people that God image was tainted by existing abuses in their family system—if dad was domineering and abusive it was likely that a) father would be feeding a child the image of a similarly abusive God-figure and b) a child would latch onto the identifying qualities of their actual father and attribute the same to a "heavenly" father.

Franciscan mystic Richard Rohr once said, "We can't love an it. We can only love a who."

Especially as children, we can't identify our belief system based on an "it"—and whether we are taught to love, hate, or fear God—it is always a "who" those feelings are directed toward. Based on the family and faith-of-origin systems, how the "who" is formed and what (inevitably) He looks like may vary some, but the God of childhood has to be human. Children and their child brains don't and can't yet reason abstractly or understand abstract symbolism like the cosmos, the universe, or the Holy Spirit. God is a man, according to most interpretations in childhood. For some, He may be a loving grandfather and for others an abusive tyrant, but either way He takes shape as human in our young minds.

In many ways, this is also the origin point of the problem later in life. As we grow into reasoning and rational creatures and as we experience pain and suffering, we see people not just in our world but in communities of faith living in ways that might conflict with what the concrete God-father described to the child minds. Most of us were taught a child's level (or spiritual kindergarten, as Richard Rohr would say) of God and spirituality, and that is where the dogma stopped. The buck stopped at doctrine, rules, and mandates for most people inside of religious traditions, and the world will never match up to the good/bad, black/white absolutes of spiritual kindergarten. The limited faith teaching most people experience mixed with the human flaws of every person—in faith communities or out—can and often will lead to some form of existential crisis, if not by overt traumatic experience, then by the growing capacity of the rational brain in adolescence and early adulthood. We are set up to be jaded if our spiritual teachings and community do not evolve past spiritual kindergarten. If people also experience abuse as their brains develop into adulthood, the religious system becomes a place of disappointing platitudes and the God figure born of a five-year-old. There is no way for this kind of a construct to hold over time. It will fall apart or be burnt down, depending on the level of hurt experienced within a person's faith community or institution.

LIFE PARABLES:
Being Hurt By Families and Faith of Origin

DAVID: For me I think the most disappointing thing all along is that I trust people, so when my leaders or mentors would disappoint or hurt me, that wounded me the most. I have this fantasy of what family should be, but because none of our families live up to the fantasy, we are always disappointed. It is the same with the church; having a fantasy about what church should be, professes to be, promises to be and experiencing the opposite—entrusting self to leaders or mentor and being hurt or betrayed by them, or experience them doing something shocking—that to me has been the most upsetting (it is because of my fantasy for what church could be—rather than dealing with reality).

DEANA: My discomfort first manifested as hunger. As a teenager I started questioning everything. Why am I here? What's the point? How am I supposed to contribute to this world? Does it even matter? Why does it matter if I believe? If belief is all that matters, why can't I go live on a mountain and be a monk?

I needed a lot more than "Stay in church, read your Bible, do your devos," which is what I had heard from church my entire life. Even when my youth pastors branched out, it was always with some sneaky version of "No sex, drugs, or rock and roll." These messages all seemed fine and good, but they turned up empty when I was having the existential crisis that is teenagehood.

KISHA: ** *trigger warning-abuse content* ** Fortunately, my theology began to evolve into something more positive during the teen years of my spiritual formation, after I experienced trauma at the hands of a couple of female mentors who sexually abused me. They were mentors whom I met at church and who were supposedly intended to be spiritual guides and/or extended family members to me. During that time, I reached out to God in the Charismatic way I had been taught, and eventually believed He met me and responded to me. However, that was not my "rebirthing" experience.

REFLECTION ON LIFE PARABLES

While church-hurt and spiritual abuse is not always about emotional, physical, and sexual trauma, or the negation of a person based on race, sexuality, and gender, there are far too many examples where this has been the case to ignore it as one of the primary sources of religious injury. To be hurt emotionally, spiritually, physically, or sexually, or negated based on the basis of who a person is, is a deep and profound wound and should be treated as such. If this is your story, it is valid and valuable. You should never be made to feel less than by someone else's mistakes—even more so, you should never be hurt in those spaces where you let your guard down the most, where abuse is done by those who are supposed to "represent" divine love on earth. There is no perfect person—and those who try to be that for others often move far off course fast. Some so far that they hurt others based on their own assumption of greatness of self. If you have been hurt by those people, there is no truth, faith, or goodness in it. It is wrong by all standards. The same is true if anyone in a faith context ever told you who you are or what you are is wrong—there is no wrong way to be and live out self and love in the world. Women are equal and good. LGBTQ people are equal and good. People of color are equal and good. If you have been told otherwise, know you are beautiful exactly as you are. Believe that truth about you. You are inherently valuable, just the way you are. No exceptions. Part of healing is believing this is true about yourself to the core—sometimes the hurt perpetrated on us creates a story we believe about ourselves. Don't believe the myth someone else has created about who you are and what you are worth—you are inherently worthy.

A HEALING PRACTICE: Faith of Origin Storytelling

PART ONE: Tell your "faith-of-origin" story. Tell it however you need to, whenever you are comfortable to do so. Answer the question asked of the interviewees in this chapter: *What was your childhood* *faith and belief of God like? How did you grow up feeling about God? How did you think God felt about you? What were the images in your mind when you pictured God? Jesus? Heaven?*

Follow up this question with one more set of questions: What was your family of origin like? Did your family/parentage resemble your God figure? If so, how? If not, how?

PART TWO: Tell the story you wish you had heard about God (if your faith of origin story was unhealthy for you). Do the same for your family of origin experience. Begin the journey toward living the life you want by creating the origin story you would have liked.

PART THREE: Create a collage of images that symbolize positive family and faith iconography and imagery. You can use any source materials—newspapers, magazines, book content—to make up your collage. Put the collage in a place you see daily; if space permits and it is comfortable for you, put it in the sacred space you created for yourself. Remember what we imagine can influence what is possible. While you can't go back to the hurtful experiences and change them, you can change your mindset in the present about how they impact you in the present. Take back your power—first in your imagination (which is where we can safely explore freedom) and then in your life.

Life Rescripting

As we discussed earlier in this chapter, we are given a script at birth, in family, and in community. We acknowledge the impression this life experience has on us, but once we see what it is and understand what it means, we can move beyond this storyline and craft the story of our future as we intend it. Sometimes we can also rescript what was into a larger narrative of our life as a whole.

This is the part of the practices where you get to be really inventive and creative.

PART ONE: First, you must remember your narrative as it is. For those of us who have lived entrenched narratives, the ones we were given, these are usually very easy to see and manifest. This is the script we play and replay year after year, over and over. This is the one we have to loosen the tether on long enough to envision something new. Initially, we must see what already exists and completely own it.

PART TWO: Second, you have to envision beyond what is and what has been to what you want your story to be. For some, this may mean releasing the old narrative; for others, it may mean embracing but being able to move beyond the old narrative into something new. Either way, the key is imagination. Imagine what you want for yourself in your life, family, or faith, what you want your story to look like—past, present, and future. Begin to tell that story. Write it down in full-color detail. Make sure to imbed all the senses—taste, smell, sight, touch, and hearing. Write your new script. Then read it out loud to yourself. Reread it as often as necessary. Work this narrative through until it is imbedded in your imagination. Then read it again.

PART THREE: The goal of this process is that you will get to a place where you can accept your history—your faith of origin and family of origin—but in a way that it is not all you are. You can see your past, present, and future, as you want to define and imagine them. Repeat the process as much or for as long as possible until you see your story as beyond the narrative you have been given and into the narrative or story you want to manifest. This is the crux of the rescripting process. It doesn't negate what was or is; it just allows for what might be with the freedom of imagination lived out in daily adult life.

CHAPTER 5

Wisdom Teachers Versus False Gurus

Save one life, you save the world. —Torah

The original sin of faith communities, leaders, or members who harm others with unloving doctrine distorts the idea of faith, God, and love. It creates a dogma of dysfunction, which then, injury by injury, taints these terms for those who they hurt. In the same way that any family abuse makes it difficult for a person to trust, so religious abuse dismantles all the same factors in both faith and literal family contexts.

It is important to understand that although the sting of religious injury is strong, it doesn't inherently mean all faith is injurious—the same way an abusive family experience doesn't mean all families are abusive. That said, there is no obligation to return to faith community after hurt—for some it is too difficult. In the steps to healing. we will explore what people choose to do after being wounded by religion. It is important, like with family abuse of any kind, to discern what is healthy and unhealthy in a spiritual or religious community, especially for those who have only experienced the abusive faith "parent." What might seem obvious to someone who has a healthy frame of reference is not always so for those who have seen little to no healthy love and family modeled for them.

Additionally, although we discuss examples from the Christian tradition—primarily because that is what my own request for hurt stories turned up—there are dangerous and insidious abuses in a variety of traditions. I have seen leaders or spiritual "parents" who are very harmful in all manner of tradition—even in yoga communities I have taken part in, and as I learned from my Buddhist teacher.

The great danger of power-abuser leaders, especially when bound to spirituality, is that they take what we want the most—meaning, belonging, and understanding—and twist it to feed their ego and need to be important. Like any abuser, they can see the vulnerabilities in people and are able to hone in on those people most in need of support and guidance, and use it to their advantage. Sadly, I have seen that kind of abuse in the most subtle and extreme forms everywhere. We all want meaning, purpose, and belonging in our lives, so without the ability to discern safe from unsafe spiritual leadership, we all can become vulnerable.

In Southeast Florida, where I currently live, there is an overwhelmingly large addiction recovery community. Something about palm trees and sunny winters created a phenomenon long ago where addiction treatment centers began heading southbound to set up their facilities in the Sunshine State. As a result, there is an extensive community of people just exiting addiction treatment living in halfway houses or independently. On any given day at any hour, you can find an AA or NA meeting somewhere within a five-mile radius of my house. In a later chapter, I will discuss the benefits of the Twelve Steps, recovery, culture, and community, but for the purposes of this chapter I am going to discuss how religious and spiritually oriented systems can manifest both the good (wisdom teacher) and the bad (false guru). This does not make a system of spirituality bad—it just means we must be watchful for all the likely places that predators, abusers, or power-hungry people might show up.

People in early recovery, especially those really willing to change their life and give their will up to a power greater than themselves, are both especially ready for transformative spirituality and particularly vulnerable to what I call the "false guru" (guru in Sanskrit means teacher). In this world, there are "wisdom teachers," and there are "false gurus." Knowing the difference between the two makes the difference between being abused for the sake of someone else's ego and finding a transformative path of healing and healthy spirituality. Unfortunately, even the healthiest people can't always know which kind of person they are encountering until they are hurt by that person. This is the intention of isolating the differences here, so perhaps the identification of the dysfunctional teacher can be seen and avoided much faster.

What I have seen in my community, among the abundance of young people in early recovery, is a deep hunger for spirituality and a strong willingness to try to explore a "power greater than" themselves. I have seen them go through amazing transformations when they encounter humble wisdom teachers, and I have seen them encounter very dangerous things when they come into contact with false gurus. In this way they are very much like all of us who are hungry and seek spiritual wisdom and divine guidance through the teachers in our midst. It is just that in these settings of increased vulnerability the false teachers rise to the top and wisdom teachers are harder to find—because true wisdom takes time and work to gain and we are a fast food faith nation, more often than not. Which means eager spiritual seekers are so easily conned by the false teachers—both those teachers that scam us through ignorance, and those that trick us with malice.

There are two particular kinds of false teachers I see most commonly—in the vulnerable places and in general (in some ways we are all in spiritually vulnerable places). The first is the unintentional false teacher—the person who genuinely believes the hurtful or dysfunctional dogma they are offering up and really believe it is helping people to be the ambassador of their doctrine. The second is more insidious—at some level this teacher knows that what they are offering is more about power than it is about belief, and they see a price tag of fame, power, or both coming to them by aligning with doctrine which will offer them this false wisdom, easily won, cheaply crafted, and sold to others at great spiritual and (often) monetary price.

This second kind of false guru is especially dangerous—they have a clear agenda that impacts anyone who is vulnerable and seeking. This faction is illustrated well in the caricature of a particular kind of yoga teacher—I have seen some version of this guy in a variety of places and faces. He is a persona and an archetype and he could just as easily be a fundamentalist teacher of any tradition, but in this case he wears tank tops rather than business suits or clericals as his uniform of swindling. I came across one recently when I landed in his yoga class without knowing his history or previously experiencing his false guru traits.. I have a clinical eye when I encounter people like him—because of my study of trauma as well as my understanding of what yoga [or insert religion here] can be when it is healthy and what it can be when it is dysfunctional in its use and application.

I walk into the class of this teacher, and his persona immediately takes up the room. He is confident with a certain pompousness that immediately makes me feel ill at ease. During the class, I noticed him lock eyes with a bunch of the younger woman, and at one point even with me. Knowing the room, like many yoga rooms in my geographical area, was filled with a number of young, vulnerable women in early recovery seeking spirituality on their mat, I was immediately suspicious of his actions. There was something inherently "car salesmany" about him. To be clinical about it—he gave me the "icks". Always trust your "icks"—they are your inner instinct trying to protect you from possible harm. Once you have been traumatized, there is that hair-raising feeling that goes deeper than trauma or traumatic response that is still calling out from deep inside to be heard.

After the class ended I went up to this teacher to ask a question—I had a Groupon I was using for the class, and I wanted to stay and see what his version of Yoga Nidra (yoga guided meditation practice) might look like—at this point more out of research and morbid curiosity as I was already suspicious of his false guru-style nature. I had to wait a few minutes because, predictably but concerningly, there were a number of young women—some of whom I knew to be in recovery—waiting to speak to him in the same eager fashion you would find for a rock star. Unfortunately, with the rise of yoga as a dominantly understood domain for Western-raised people seeking Eastern-style spirituality, there can be a misunderstanding that because someone teaches yoga, he or she must have insight into some deeper and more transformative wisdom. This is no more true of every teacher or studio owner than it might be of every therapist or clergy member. As in all other arenas, there are healthy leaders and wisdom teachers, and there are dysfunctional/abusive leaders and false gurus.

As he talked to these young women, he got uncomfortably close to them, his language full of platitudes and complements, and his eye contact ravenous as he gazed into their eyes, almost without blinking.

Once the small crowd dissipated, I went up to ask my question. "Excuse me. I am staying for the Yoga Nidra. Do I need to sign in again for the next session?"

He looked at me uncomfortably long, moved into my personal space and gazed in his unblinking fashion and said, "Did you see during class that moment? We locked eyes and in the breath, we had that moment. Did you feel it?"

Inner Ick! My question was matter of fact and simple. I gave no inclination with my body language or verbal language that I was seeking anything else, but there he was running his game on me.

With my skin crawling, I replied, "Sure. So do I need to sign in again?"

He touched my arm and said, "It was really a powerful moment… No, you don't have to sign in. Get comfortable for the meditation. It is a spiritually powerful experience. People who have done my Yoga Nidra have had some of their greatest dreams and visions come true."

To which my inner reply was a sardonic, "Ok."

My outer reply was to move my mat into the back, grit my teeth, and try to get through this investigative meditation—at this point I wanted to see how far his dysfunctional false guru nature went. He did not disappoint. His meditation was full of all kinds of platitudes, promises, and allure—just enough to rope in anyone who was wounded or seeking who hadn't seen his kind before. He promised people great things from his meditation—wish-fulfillment spirituality, which in any tradition is the most superficial and disappointing kind. I hate being right about those kinds of people in my midst—but I was about him. He was a false guru to the core, and he still teaches and runs his own studio. This is terrifying. I do my best, in my community and elsewhere, to teach people about the nature of a false guru—so that fewer people are likely to fall for this kind of carnival trickery and smoke-and-mirrors faith.

For those of you outside of this particular spiritual community or culture, you can insert any abusive leaders you have encountered—they are the same in certain traits. They just wear different clothing and outfits of convincing, but they are all innately and alarmingly similar. They also know how to find those who are the most seeking and use their vulnerability and spiritual aspiration against them, for their own purposes.

Unmasking the False Guru

There are a number of quintessential characteristics and methodologies of the false guru. Whether this might help you in looking backward to those who hurt or abused you in a faith context, or in moving forward to isolate the characteristics to investigate in your own life experience, use this template (and build in your own discoveries) to see those leaders who use their role to build themselves up and keep others bound to them. This is similar to family codependency but sometimes even more dangerous because it binds you in relationship to them and keeps them as a conduit to your own spiritual path.

1. **Certitude and Extreme Confidence**: They are so sure of themselves and their version of teachings, and their brand of wisdom. They question almost nothing about themselves, their lives, or their beliefs. If there is any humility, it is often loud and dramatic—all about the pomp and show of it, the kind of show put on by someone who doesn't understand the definition of actual humility.

2. **Charisma and Charm Overdose**: They are super suave, well dressed (in whatever that looks like for their tradition), and so alluring. Their smile, stare, and smoothness of speech is almost hypnotically alluring—and the more vulnerable you are, the more you are prey to this kind of allure.

3. **Promises and Wish Fulfillment**: Their brand of spirituality, religion, or dogma is going to get you everything you want—no more pain, loss, or poverty (literal or emotional). All your dreams will come true—and if they don't, it means you are doing something wrong, not them. You aren't true enough in your belief—that is what they will tell you.

4. **The Golden Ticket Rule:** Like Willy Wonka—they have the golden ticket to your happiness, afterlife, and spiritual journey, and there is a limited supply. But conjoint with the wish fulfillment, if you stick with them, they can help you attain it.

5. **The Price Tag:** This is not true of all false gurus, but often there is a hefty price tag for their brand of enlightenment or exclusive members-only afterlife. If it costs a lot to get to Nirvana, then it probably isn't Nirvana.

6. **The Pyramid Scheme and Isolation:** They want you to invite your friends to join this community—bring them in—but you can't spend much time outside the community to see them. Your life must revolve around this community, teachings, members, and most importantly, its leader. You are taught that if you really loved your friends you would bring them in—if they don't follow, then they aren't the right friends for you anyway.

7. **This Way Is the Only Way:** Building on the isolation tactics—this way, this teacher, their teaching—is the way to get all that you want. Every other way to spiritual wholeness or faith is just not as good or potentially totally wrong. There is no ambiguity—we are right and we are best, so why go anywhere else?

8. **No Room for Open-Ended Questions or Interpretations:** If your question is to the leader to ask him or her what you should do, think, or believe, then that is ok. If you question or disagree with what is said, then you will be made to feel less than or like you don't "get it." There is no room for ambiguity with false gurus—because that means you might begin to question, and that wouldn't work for their agenda.

9. **Narcissism or Sociopathic Tendencies:** Psychologically this kind of a personality has at least some traits of clinical narcissism—their confidence exudes from that place of buying their own greatness. In more extreme scenarios, they may also have some or all traits of sociopathy. Simply put, sociopathy is an incapacity for human emotion, which means they don't feel the hurts they impose on others. This makes the manipulation they use easy for them to do as they have no capacity for remorse. Not all false guru leaders are sociopaths, but most will fall somewhere on the spectrum between narcissism and sociopathy.

10. **They Are Above the World and Its Rules:** Part of the reason that many of these type of leaders are the ones who end up in the headlines is because their ego is so big and their understanding of reality outside of themselves (especially as their power grows) is so distorted that they begin to believe what they are selling to the point that they think they are above reproach. Because they often have at least some traits of narcissism and the most extreme would probably fit on the spectrum for sociopathy, they will push the limits, and most end up doing something

societally illegal because they truly believe they are above crime and reproach. This might include any or all of the following—stealing or appropriating community funds into their own accounts, sexual misconduct or even abuse, and being verbally and emotionally abusive of its members or leaders below them in their hierarchy).

The above list is not exhaustive, and a false guru might not exhibit all these traits, but it is important to know what to look for to see the difference between healthy spirituality and leadership and that which is destructive and abusive. If you are a spiritual seeker on a path of self-discovery (in religion or out), you deserve to have teachers who are wise and humble along your journey. You deserve to be nurtured—and the above personality doesn't know how to do that. In truth, it is not even their intention. Their intention is to improve their value and esteem, not to help you grow.

Identifying the Wisdom Teacher

We could say that to discover a true wisdom teacher philosophically and religiously, just pick the opposite of the false guru and you are in good starting shape. That said, I want to be specific about what the alternative to the false guru looks like. We all deserve at least one good teacher to learn from, especially when it comes to spirituality and philosophical understanding. If you are looking for a teacher, have been hurt before but want to explore the spiritual or philosophical complexities of life, and/or want to find faith that embraces the unknown, then this listing of traits of healthy teachers is a starting point for your journey.

1. **Humility over Ego:** Wisdom Teachers promote humility in others and most importantly, in themselves. They are always part of community and offer their teachings as learned lessons along the way. Their teachings are not based on their own value or "better than others" nature. In community they make sure there are checks and balances to make sure that if their ego begins to appear, there is an accountability system to ensure they come back down to earth and explore any issues of narcissism.

2. **Community over Themselves:** While they may be wisdom teachers with experience and knowledge, they do not think of themselves as most important. They want to bring the strengths,

values, creativity, and wisdom of the community together for a more diverse and strong whole—rather than a leader-based, top-down system of power with themselves at the top. They are attentive to creating balance and avoiding power and control roles or characteristics.

3. **Embracing the Tension:** They offer their teachings and life lessons to others but are also able to accept when outside realities or ideas may contrast with what they have learned— they can hold the tension between what they know and don't know, between their truth and the truth as seen through others' eyes, and between being wise and needing to learn and grow themselves.

4. **Comfortable with the Unknown:** One of the essential characteristics of wisdom teachers is that they know enough to realize that the universe, cosmos, God, and/or the ineffable can only be understood in a very small portion. They understand that a lifetime of education can only touch the surface of understanding God/the universe/their higher power.

5. **They Are Lifelong Students:** They are willing and open to sharing that much of spirituality, and faith is unknown and unknowable—and that they, as teachers, still have much to learn as students themselves. They constantly engage with the unknown through meditation, sacred practices, and other wisdom teachers. They understand that learning, growth, and transformation is a lifelong process and are willing to engage with that process for the duration of their own lives.

6. **Promote Questions and Don't Have All the Answers:** They don't pretend to have all the answers and are willing to say, "I don't know," or "Let me find out more about that and get back to you." They believe that human curiosity is a gift and nurture that curiosity and the art of asking questions in others. They want people to question and explore deeper.

7. **Low- to No-Cost Teachings:** Although some elements of their teachings and programming might have a cost, it is the lowest cost possible, includes many scholarships for those who can't afford it, and offers most of what they do for free or as close to free as possible. Of course, overhead for certain things require cost, but wisdom teachers are not getting rich and buying mansions off of their work.

8. **Accepting of Many Ways to Transformation and Spirituality:** True wisdom teachers don't believe their way, tradition, or understanding of the universe is the only one—they are open to many paths to the same source. This is a very contemplative dimension of thinking about the world and engages with the nondual nature of things—meaning that one person, faith, or path doesn't have to be wrong for another to be right. They don't see the world as an either-or proposition, but rather a series of trails, which lead to the same loving source—whatever that central source of all things might be called or how it might be defined.

9. **Promote Radical Inclusion:** They believe that everyone and everything belongs—and we all should have the opportunity to find happiness, love, and understanding. This means that outside of just seeing spirituality or faith as an independent personal journey or a journey for one community alone, that we all walk together, have to care for one another, and open our homes, hearts, and faith to all. This can mean not excluding people from their work or world or value them less because of their race, gender, sexuality, socioeconomic status, or global location.

10. **Model Unconditional Love and Forgiveness:** They believe everyone deserves love, and that love is not conditional on any of the above factors being a certain way. Love is love, and everyone gets the same portion—with no strings attached. They also believe that if a person has done wrong, then they deserve forgiveness—as much for the one offering forgiveness as for the other person. They believe in paths to reconciliation as the answer to conflict, strife, and marginalization of people. That doesn't mean there is no justice, just that justice is found with loving compassion. They see justice as a difficult path, and one done with a transformed and loving heart is the way to find true personal and collective healing. They model this in their life and works and seek outside input if they get stuck in jadedness and hate.

11. **Acknowledge Their Own Flawed Humanity:** They admit they make mistakes and when they do, they try to be transparent about them and share their hurt and falls as a way to help others learn and grow. They don't hide their mistakes—they use them to help themselves and others get back up after the falls.

12. **Value Independence and Uniqueness Along with Healthy Interdependence:** They believe in the inherent value of community for opportunities to show unconditional love, work through relationship for authentic companionship, and provide accountability for themselves and others. They also value each person and their unique set of talents, history of hurt, and all that makes them who they are—and they honor that person and all their parts in community.

13. **Authenticity:** They are who they are—without a hidden agenda or secret parts. They work toward deeper authenticity and promote others to do the same. They believe we are all flawed and beautiful.

Just as with the false guru teacher, this wisdom teacher reference is not comprehensive, but it is a guide post—if you find people along your own healing path and spiritual or philosophical journey with these traits, then they may be people to spend more time with. Discern in your own life the wisdom teachers of your story—if they follow the above path in some form, they are someone we can all learn from. Since they are open to their own ever-evolving path, they might just learn something from you, too.

CHAPTER 6

Peeling the Onion

Religious Injury Subtypes

Humility...is nothing else but a true knowledge and experience of yourself as you are. —The Cloud of Unknowing

This topic of religious wounds and church-hurt has been percolating as an increasingly louder conversation for at least the better part of 10 years, although the last five have been when I have seen major changes in the form of dialogue about it. There are more Facebook groups, support groups, and personal stories being shared in the wider virtual and literal public squares in and out of faith contexts than ever before. However, since the concept is very new as an area of study, and definitely has had minimal assessment and treatment within the wider field of traumatology, it seems appropriate to break down the varieties of religious trauma to different types of abuse and traumatic experience. This categorization, much like this book as a whole, is a means to speak into the pain with a few tangible concepts, so that those who have been hurt can feel heard and validated, so those who hope to support them personally or as a clinical provider can understand this trauma better, and perhaps the loftiest aspiration, so those in faith communities can understand why many people have left faith communities and find ways to nurture rather than retraumatize survivors of religious trauma.

To change something, we must first understand what it is and where it lies inside both our society and ourselves. A few additional terms will be explored in this chapter. including internalized oppression, attachment issues as they related to religious abuses, and other relevant areas of discussion. We will also explore a number of situations and people groups where historic and pervasive abuse and neglect have occurred in religious contexts. Does this mean every religious context contains these abuses? No. In taking on the task to write this book and still exist within both secular clinical and faith-based contexts, I have found a strange double bind. People untrusting of religion have a hard time believing I don't have a proselytizing ulterior motive (mistrust is often, understandably, a symptom of the pain of trauma), and many religious folks have seen me as some kind of fraudulent interloper, there to prove that religion is bad.

While neither are true, I would say it has tested my ability to hold the tension between two widely separated spaces and hurt places, as well as hold my own historical religious prickly places in check—and remember that on either side of trauma and misunderstanding there is fear and self-protection inherent to how we hold ourselves and our psyches together. I do it. We all do it. I knew moving into this project that I would face my own religious history of hurts, and I would have to face those on both sides of this experience who would question my motives. But this is my only goal: I want to bring religious wounds and church-hurt out of the darkness of shame and silence and into the light so we can all see how we might validate this trauma—religiously, psychologically, and secularly—and find a way to move beyond hurt and pain into something transformed as people and as communities. I hope this preliminary review of trauma in religious contexts will help manifest such a dialogue.

Sexual and Physical Abuse

Sexual and physical abuse, primarily by religious leaders, is the most well-known form of trauma in a religious context. There can be many ways that an oppressive system can collaborate with abuses that happen under their roof, by silence, denial, or self-preserving untruths. Before we get into those specifics, I want to clarify a point I often see misinterpreted or misunderstood.

Something I have seen consistently assumed, most prominently related to the Catholic Church when a scandal occurs or a clergy sexual predator is discovered, is that priests are somehow more dominant sexual predators than any other people group, or that all priests have an inherent dysfunctional and abusive behavior. I can understand, outside of a trauma-based perspective, how this could be an immediate assumption—based on the number and prominence of these cases uncovered in the last decade or so. I have seen similar conclusions jumped to when I would discuss my work with survivors of military sexual trauma—first, it would be assumed that all the victims were female, and second, that the kind of people and training that occurs in a military context creates sexual predators. Neither was inherently true, and the same should be understood for predators in religious contexts or by clergypersons. To understand the nature of sexual predators in systems of power, namely in religion, it is important to see what is true and what is myth/ We have to see clearly without assumptions or misgivings, before we can even begin to heal as persons and communities.

Power-seeking predators (sexual or otherwise) look for places where their predatory nature will be most easily disguised and least likely discovered. Any system built on a hierarchical structure, where there are roles of power or authority, will be places sought out by predators—but this is much different than saying all people who end up in systems or positions of power and authority are or will be predators—sexually, physically, or emotionally. The difficulty is that predators are clever and know they thrive best in systems that are structured to protect power and give victims little room for recourse. This is why we see abuses such as these in places like religion and the military—the nature of the structure is inherently protective of the person(s) with more power. This is the dynamic we need to be careful of and critique, not necessarily just the roles of authority in and of themselves, but to make sure we find ways to create more transparency in those structures for the safety of all involved. If we were to compare religion and the military, we can actually find a number of corollaries between them as systems of power and authority. Due to recent scandals and focus on sexual assault in the military, it is doing a better job at transparency and creating an external system of checks and balances when there is abuse in the ranks. Far from perfect, the military may be a few steps ahead of the religious systems in creating methods to correct this systemic shield that was once in place to (intentionally or no)t protect the predator rather than the victims.

If we can be clear from the start that all people in positions of power are not inherently abusers or sexual predators, then we can then dig deeper to see the systemic issues that can protect predators in systems—specifically religious systems.

Sexual and physical abuse in a religious context can be very damaging, and because of a systemic hierarchy, combined with the authority of God as the "boss" of those people in power, the control a predator in religion has over those they victimize is immense—even more than in most systems. The correlating shame and silencing imposed on the victim is multiplied because there is a system of power (purportedly) led by God, which is facilitating this abuse. The perpetrators in religious systems are very clever and make sure those they are abusing believe they have no recourse or self-esteem to speak up. It is a cruel brutalization at all levels and impacts everything from a person's sense of worthiness, lovability, "sinfulness" or goodness, and can make it feel like there is no way out. To exit such an experience in a religious system takes a lot of courage—and it is equally understandable why so many people remain stuck in those abusive situations. Hopefully, the more people speak out about this issue, and the more voices that are heard (anonymously or not), the easier it will become for people to exit these abusive systems.

Sometimes the abuser is the "leader" of a household, sometimes they are a "leader" in the church structure, and often they are both. If you have been abused physically and sexually in a religious community, it is not your fault. You didn't ask for or deserve it or any other negative statement or belief your abuser wants you to believe. There are places to escape and sources of help—domestic violence shelters, child protective agencies, therapists and crisis providers outside the community system. You do not deserve any abuse you ever received. You should know that before all else whether you are in or outside of an abuse situation. You did not deserve it. You are inherently good. You can heal from this pain—although in the worst moments it is hard to believe.

LIFE PARABLES

DEB: I will start with one that has plagued me my whole life. My brother's godfather was a deacon in our church. His wife was also our caretaker after school and on the weekends because my mother had to work extra hours to make up for my father's irresponsible spending. While I was at their house, I was sexually abused by this man and his son on separate occasions. I don't know if the one knew the other was doing it, and his son was probably about 12 when it started. My first memory of it was when I was three years old. I know I was three because my brother was still in a carrier, and I was three when he was born. The abuse may or may not have occurred in the church. My memory is fuzzy on that, and I am undergoing Eye Movement Desensitization and Rreprocessing (EMDR) therapy to remedy that. The abuse continued until 1994, when we moved to Florida. I told my mother a few months later, and she informed the Assemblies of God, who did *nothing* but remove him as a deacon. At age 17, I confronted him in the church when I was sent back to Connecticut on vacation/punishment to be with my grandmother for the summer. The meeting was between the two abusers, the pastor of the church at the time, who happened to be my mother's ex-boyfriend, my grandmother, and my uncle. The abusers vehemently denied any wrongdoing, and I spent the time being so angry at them while others watched and did nothing.

Other experiences included seeing my mother being stripped of her singing privileges after an affair she had with another man. This happened even though I knew that my father had many girlfriends yet was still able to play in the band. My mother's beautiful voice was taken away from the congregation.

My father was also very physically abusive, and after EMDR therapy, I have finally determined that he was also sexually abusive also. I remember going to my aunt with this accusation. She is a minister and always told me I was probably mistaking my father for the other abusers, and it was just a dream. I just found out several months ago that it was not, in fact, a dream.

KISHA: I experienced trauma at the hands of a couple of my female mentors who sexually abused me. They were mentors whom I met at church who were supposedly intended to be some sort of spiritual guides and/or extended family members to me. During that time up until approximately a year-and-a-half ago, I carried around deep shame, confusion, insecurity, and inappropriate guilt regarding my sexuality. For many years, I wasn't exactly sure who I was, what I wanted sexually, nor what was ok for me to want. I was confused about the identity of Jesus, because my faith tradition is a "Oneness" tradition that always combined the identities of both God and Jesus as one in the same. Therefore, I thought they both hated me in unison. My view of Heaven was merely that it was a place that I would probably never see. I believed that if I were to see it, I would first have to stand in line naked waiting to be judged on Judgment Day. I worried that everybody in line would see my naked body, and that even in Heaven, I would have to go around naked with no clothes, no privacy, and no boundaries. I was deeply ashamed of my body.

Secondary Traumatic Stress (from religious abuse)

We discussed secondary stress a bit earlier and defined it as stress that comes from someone in relationship with persons who have been abused or those who hear the accounts of abuse. This is an exhausting role and one not often seen or recognized as such. Recently, with the burgeoning use of virtual networks and social media, I am seeing this happen virtually as well. People or community groups built to support survivors of religious injury or abuse are becoming overwhelmed with the sheer number of stories coming into these virtual spaces from facilitators of these intended safe web spaces and other community members. People are getting fried on hearing others' hurt.

This doesn't mean we shouldn't confide in loved ones, care providers, or virtual communities, but it does mean that if you are someone absorbing the experiences of others' trauma, you have to be aware this can impact your own well-being. A brief example comes from my early experience as a therapist intern with combat veterans. I had my own history of trauma and my own PTSD healing when I landed my first graduate internship. I felt that although the experiences of my clients were traumatic, they were so far away from anything I could relate to that the likelihood of it impacting me was slim. Slowly, in a way I didn't even see at first by hearing trauma accounts all day, I began absorbing the content and emotional dimensions of their stories, and they became a part of me. I began experiencing symptoms that had nothing to do with my own traumatic experience but were related to my clients' trauma. I would swerve when I saw garbage on the side of the road—a typical combat trauma response of Iraq veterans due to the number of improvised explosive devices (IEDs) in the combat zone. I would wake up from night terrors full of bullets flying and explosions—where I would be injured in the middle of a combat zone. I began appropriating an exaggerated startle response, especially when people came up behind me—something I had all but rid myself of in my own trauma recovery. It was a few weeks into this before I saw the connection—I was manifesting the symptoms of PTSD for the combat veterans who were my therapy clients. Since then I have learned to curate boundaries that diminish the likelihood of that happening—but there is always the random occasion, over the years, where a particular story or experience will linger with me. So if you are a loved one, community member, or helping professional seeking to support those who have experienced trauma in a religious context, know that self-care and boundaries are as important for you as for the survivor. The way you help people best is by taking care of yourself enough to have the stamina for the long haul. This is a form of traumatization and, at some point, it can be helpful to get your own support system, support group, and/or therapy provider to help you address your own traumatic experience.

This kind of traumatic experience can often lead to the issues mentioned above—appropriate the symptoms of another person, as well as issues of anxiety, anger, or general emotional overwhelmingness. Depending on how overwhelming it is, it can commonly be moderated by emotional numbing to desensitize the self from the pain of others.

Gender Identity Negation

The use of religious texts to validate one set of people and negate another is something religious traditions in their worst forms have been doing forever. Being a woman in a great many versions of religious traditions can be varying shades of a negative personal trait. It can limit what you can do in a religious community and culture, if you are allowed to talk and what you are allowed to say or are considered capable of saying. Your station can be low and limited in a way that much of contemporary society might consider gender dynamics of the 1800s. This is seen again as a theme in issues of historic abuse and colonization, sexual identity negation, and more.

If we go back to the inherent dynamics of power and privilege in hierarchies, we can see abuses of some by others pursuing power. Selecting a "lesser" gender, or at the very least a passive and silent gender, is one way to rule out any fight for power from about half of any community group.

Even though it may not feel healthy or right, even when women leave communities that devalue them just for being a woman, it is hard to get rid of the inherent "not enough" feeling percolating deep inside. It also makes it difficult for women to claim all manner of their lives and selfhood—including their bodies, sexuality, strengths, and abilities. It is a sort of brainwashing and programming, happening through the childhood growth and development cycles into adulthood, and becomes very ingrained. Even when a woman can leave that belief system and begin to gain some sense of autonomy, it takes time and work to deprogram her own inwardly driven sense of being less than a man.

This version of traumatic experience can lead to issues of anxiety, shame/guilt, anger (often self-inflicted both emotionally and possibly physically through cutting or eating disorders), and grief and loss. This is not all, but these are some common manifestations. The anger is usually inwardly driven at first due to the learned behavior of not letting opinions, feelings, and selfhood be expressed externally from the faith tradition that negated them.

LIFE PARABLE: Kisha

In addition to carrying deep trauma and shame surrounding my sexuality, I also carried shame regarding my gender. I come from a very musical family. I also come from a very Levitical family. In spite of my gifts for singing, playing instruments, and preaching, I was never encouraged, trained, or allowed to use any of them in the church because those opportunities were only given to boys. There existed a glass ceiling for girls and women within the church that was rarely ever spoken about, but always implied and definitely understood. For the few women who were somehow granted opportunities for leadership within the church, there was so much competition that many of them ended up leaving the church and starting their own ministries elsewhere. Meanwhile I was left stuck with no motivation to practice, sharpen, or appreciate my ministry gifts. I saw no point. They would never be valuable anyway.

Sexual Identity Negation

Sexual identity negation is another powerfully painful way unhealthy or abusive religious communities and religious doctrine can negate and devalue a person based on who they are as a human being. Due to the extreme doctrinal statements about being LGBTQ (lesbian, gay, bisexual, transgendered, queer) by many extreme forms of many religions, it can also be physically dangerous to be openly LGBTQ in certain communities. There are many people in these traditions who live closeted and in fear as a means of self-preservation. The alternative could mean losing family, friends, and entire community group indefinitely if not permanently. That is a lot to give up, so many still function in these communities as much or as long as they can. There is no wrong choice in these situations—each one is difficult. If people stay closeted in a community, they lose access to an intrinsic part of who they are; if they leave, then they may lose everyone they have ever known and loved.

The difficulty unique to LGBTQ people in abusive faith cultures, different from gender issues, is that who the person is while in that community is a secret. A woman is a woman, and that is a visible fact—even when it is diminished or abused by the community, her gender is open. For someone who is LGBTQ, the love of their family and community can feel especially fragile and conditional—they know that if they come out, that love can be rescinded, and their nature touted as wrong or sinful. If you are not LGBTQ, imagine for a moment that who you are is considered a sin—as you are when you were born, as you are when you die. Imagine for a moment that your very life was considered sinful—that is an excruciating thing to bear.

It is no wonder that LGBTQ persons, if they leave their faith tradition, can find it difficult to ever return to another faith community—fearing the possible lack of acceptance they experienced in their faith of origin. Some of the common issues from religious trauma experienced by LGBTQ persons are shame/guilt built in from a negating religious community, anxiety, isolation, and trust/intimacy issues due to fear of rejection.

LIFE PARABLE: Marg

At 16 years old, I had come to realize I was a lesbian. My best friend from church and I had fallen in love with each other. Our love felt so pure, so tender, and so holy that I knew being gay was not a bad thing. But it was 1979, and you couldn't be gay and Christian both. Yet, there we were. One day, when I was 18, I told the current youth minister at church that I was gay. I don't know why I thought nothing would change. Maybe because it was I, and it was my church, I had grown up there, and I was safe there. But I was wrong. I misread him, and I misunderstood the times. The first thing he said was, "Well, you won't be able to work with the children anymore." I had been working with the younger kids for 10 years, more than half my life, likely longer than he had. At first I was stunned. But then an awful realization came over me. Uttering two words, "I'm gay," had twisted my reality on its axis. The minister would never trust me again. I had changed. In five seconds I had become a sexual offender, a sinner going to hell. Church was no longer safe for someone like me.

Soon after that day, I left. I left the building, the people, the music, and the memories. I left what I thought would be the setting for the rest of my life. I left.

LIFE PARABLE: Tim

...So I developed my faith and sexuality along the lines of what I'd been told since there weren't any alternatives presented. For some reason, it was quite easy to "control myself" around girls, but I ended up getting crushes and dated a few times. I was genuinely attracted to a number of my female friends. But the sex drive I'd been warned about seemed easy, or at least possible, to control around women. (In hindsight, this was probably a result of training, morals, and inexperience. And perhaps having other options! One good thing: it kept me out of trouble...)

But I also experienced crushes and "uncontrollable" feelings for the occasional guy. I then ended up in situations in which I was curious, and things went further than I expected. Ironically, the church training about "keeping safe" around women left me woefully unprepared for navigating these experiences. So there was no one I could talk to, and I felt terribly guilty. I had no role models for healthy homosexual relationships, and people I trusted handled it very badly. So I felt increasingly guilty, and because of that guilt, kept Jesus a long way away from that part of my life. Then I discovered Internet pornography, and it was obvious that I was interested in homosexual pornography. I felt excruciatingly guilty, but, in hindsight, it was mainly driven by curiosity about a world I had never experienced, that I didn't even have words for, yet was somehow a part of me. It was an outlet for feelings I couldn't talk about, or even name. So in my public persona, I was straight by default. There just weren't any other viable options socially, intellectually, or "biblically". But in private, I was trying to work out how to navigate a world where I had homosexual desires, and I was trying to hide that fact from myself and suppress those desires. I used to feel Jesus could never love me while I continued to make serious errors, whether I wanted to do these things, or whether I avoided them. (Yes, I had an internal hierarchy of sins.) In particular, I felt that Jesus could never love me while I was attracted to men (among many things not ideal, perfect, and complete in my life.) This led me to feel fear, guilt, and rejection at my core. I could certainly never accept myself in this situation, and I could never entirely be at peace, whatever I told myself about God's love. The condemnation of particular aspects of my life was much clearer than Jesus' love for everyone, whatever their circumstances. While there was obvious pressure to change and conform, I did not feel accepted by Jesus, let alone the church. I had also tried very hard to change my sexual orientation over that decade. I'd had several attempts at counseling, online courses, prayer, behavioral modification, confession, spiritual warfare, and almost anything else I could think of. But nothing worked, at least not for more than a year, or so, at a time. It just made it that much harder to process my sexual orientation, as I am not just bisexual, but fluid in my degree of attraction to masculinity and femininity. It was that fluidity that confused the issue, because I would seem to go straight for a while, but it would never last. And I hated tying the success of my faith to my feelings for men. I didn't even have a functional concept of bisexuality until the last few years. Before that, it just wasn't something I could imagine myself being: I had always thought of myself as a straight guy with a "gay problem." These weren't the only issues I thought of during this time (I had a lot of thinking time). I struggled with how the church functioned for the physically disabled; the not stereotypically masculine "men"; the nonneurotypical (whether autistic or more broadly mentally differing); and, as I have already mentioned, the "not straight." I struggled with my own experiences of each of these, and I felt trapped to hear that I had been part of what was considered to be negative characteristics: I become quite critical, bitter, angry, frustrated, and demanding.

Intergenerational and Historic Trauma

Intergenerational trauma is the traumatic experience that spans more than one generation or one lifetime and for which the impact compounds and grows through the generations. It is handed down in memories, in behaviors of elder generations, and possibly even, as we are learning more recently, in genetic code and DNA. Some examples of intergenerational trauma would be generations following Holocaust survivors, combat veterans, and in the cultural context, family lineage of marginalized or colonized community groups—most prominently seen in Native American communities but potentially any community with marginalized people or persons of color.

The way this can manifest is multifaceted. When we are discussing issues of colonized or marginalized persons, this can express itself in a variety of social and dynamics, as well as with issues of internalized oppression. Internalized oppression happens when people appropriate a sense of internal self from outward cultural and social negatives about themselves and their people group. In many ways all the symptoms of trauma are internalized abuse—in the sense that the abusing system or person(s) provided a framework to devalue and abuse people in a religious context, and the symptoms are often an inward expression of that outward belief imposed on that person by the abusers. In some ways we can look at all religious trauma as a form of internalized oppression—even if it is not in the traditional way we look at oppression. Religious trauma is a form of oppression— oppressing people and their human traits, beliefs, and beyond—to build up the power and value of people at the top of a hierarchical system.

Intergenerational trauma can express itself as repeating cycles of abuse and being abused, addiction and low self-worth, and potentially rage, anxiety, and guilt. It is especially profound for those who have felt mutually marginalized by society and by church/faith communities (as is discussed further in the racial and cultural trauma section below).

...And Racial and Cultural Identity Trauma

Racial and cultural identity trauma relates to intergenerational trauma when it is experienced among marginalized communities in the sense that it is the experience of being lesser than the dominant culture of the church system. This can be obviously or subtly felt. As Bill, articulates in his story, just the experience of having to show up to a church gathering where dress attire is expected can be a way to demean those who might not have the economic means to dress that way. Also insensitive discussions or actions around issues of race or cultural differences can be especially piercing. Even though intellectually we can say that church is made up of people and therefore will inherently include human mistakes and prejudices, we want to expect more of places that articulate a standard of caring for one another, so it is especially painful when those communities let us down.

This kind of trauma can lead to issues of shame and guilt, low self-esteem, anger, rage, and isolation. It can be hard for people who have been marginalized, such as in their church communities, to trust other community groups and personal relationships. It is important to validate this as real traumatic experience and to hold communities accountable to rectifying the margins as well as raising their own standards for how to care for others.

LIFE PARABLE: Emma

The intergenerational trauma for me with the Church was related to the overall culture of the community's racism. When I was growing up, we kind of accepted the racism in my church and community. It was kind of weird. There was a lot of racism, but I didn't understand just how much until I moved away from home and looked at other communities. In my small town it was blatant, in your face. You would feel you needed to dress up just to go shopping, whereas if you were Non-Native or not a person of color, you wouldn't feel that need. I knew the feeling of someone following you around in a store. Moving away from my Native Church into a Non-Native church definitely tied into my beliefs of Christianity too. We didn't have the church we were comfortable going to, and it was difficult after our warrior mascot protests with the Non-Native church in our town. After we had stood up in front of our school and town in protest of a Native American symbol as a mascot it went from just being a minority person to being someone who was unwanted by our community—including and especially our church. You could tell we were not welcome anymore. We got a scholarship from church when we were leaving high school and it felt like they were saying, "We are doing the right thing, but we don't want to." They gave us the scholarship because we were confirmed, and the Non-Native girl who applied for it was not. They made sure to let us know that was the only reason why we got it.

This church alienation was surrounded by all of the cultural, racial, and intergenerational trauma issues. Back in my community in South Dakota, there are no resources, and they are just starting to get more with passing the Violence Against Women Act (VAWA). Before that, there wasn't anything—you didn't feel safe. Being a teenager growing up in a racist community where you know nothing will be done for any wrongdoing against you is very sad. In our town, if you go to court, there are only Native people there—that says a lot. With the trauma I have been through, our decision to protest the warrior mascot and the coronation ceremony for four years (doing what we thought was right) was a lot to take on. That same year we started protesting, I was sexually assaulted, and that erased entirely the ability to feel safe in my own town. During the protests, we had a lot of the people who came to help us—people connected to the Lakota Student Alliance and others connected with the American Indian Movement (AIM). They knew how dangerous the community was, but we didn't. A lot of them had been through the Wounded Knee Occupation as children, but we hadn't. We were just trying to do the right thing. They came in to would warn us and say you need to smudge with sage (a Native protection practice) before you leave the house and when you come back. They were right because friends were warning us to not go to this party or to that school event because the community was planning to do something to us. One time they told us not to go to a bonfire—as cheerleaders we were supposed to be there—because the community members/students were going to stone us. My hope is that there are always people helping, so people can work on themselves enough to realize there are so many other people who are hurting too. I have seen that a lot in community. We are seeing there are so many people who need healing and don't even realize it. Now that I understand more about my traumas, as well as intergenerational trauma and how trauma can get passed in the DNA, I understand myself much better. No wonder why my feelings are so overwhelming to me; they are related to my ancestors too. A lot of times now when things get overwhelming, I can see where it is coming from.

Family (of Religious) Systems Trauma

In therapy, we call the work with and issues of families "family systems" work. In families of unhealthy or abusive religion, as described in the previous family and trauma chapter, the unhealthy family system bleeds together with the unhealthy religious system to compound the impact on a person. As previously described, if the household "father" and the church "father" come together to injure, marginalize, or diminish a person, and state that this injury is actually a mandate from the holy "father," this is a very difficult system to unwind—it is triple the trauma and triple the hurt. It is hard enough to work through family traumatic experience with someone because it means dismantling everything they learned from their first breaths about love, themselves, and what it means to be safe (or unloved, invalid, and unsafe). When we are dealing with family trauma inside a faith system of trauma and you throw in the dysfunctional image of God created by both systems, it takes a lot of time and work to undo. It is not impossible, but the complexity of it means it takes time.

LIFE PARABLE: David

For me, I think the most disappointing thing all along is that I trusted people, so when my leaders or mentors (I was a pastor for many years), would disappoint or hurt me. that wounded me the most. I have this fantasy of what family should be, and because none of our families live up to the fantasy, we are always disappointed. Often it is the same with the church. We have a fantasy of what church professes and promises to be, and yet we experience the opposite. You entrust yourself to leaders or mentors, and if they hurt or betray you or do something shocking—that has been the most upsetting to me. In my childhood fantasy of what church could be, God looked exactly like my father. I still see an old man sitting on a throne in the clouds. I associated God with father. My dad was a strong disciplinarian, and I saw God that way—as strict. Jesus was more like a buddy, so I maintained my spiritual life through Jesus and by being obedient to God at the same time. I was afraid of father and didn't want to make him angry so I was obedient, but inwardly screaming.

LIFE PARABLE: Anonymous

The saddest part of my experience is that I didn't realize my spiritual experiences had created wounds until I was in my 40s. I was born into an evangelical, charismatic family whose religious affiliation was a group that was cult-like in their approach. In other words, the group believed in God, the Divinity, atonement of Jesus, the Resurrection, and ministry of the Holy Spirit ... so far, so good (kind of). But then there were layers and sublayers. For example, "established churches," as they called those groups who meet regularly in designated church buildings, were deceived and not "true Christians". Anyone who didn't worship with us, in the format we considered right, was deceived and not really Christian at all. As in most evangelical groups, the concept of the doctrine of original sin was one of the foundational tenets. Everything was based on how bad humans are, and how important it is to subdue their pervasive sin nature and achieve holiness. Holiness was manifested in behavior—right clothing (restrictions were heaviest on females), right appearances (attendance at thrice-weekly, multiple-hour services), right economics (owning very little outright, sharing of all resources communally, not possessing anything "too nice"), right observations (no "pagan" holidays, which basically meant no observing of any date, although birthdays were considered "okay if you must") ... and the list went on. Thus my childhood understanding of God was that He didn't like me very much, even though He loved me (which made no sense to me, so what stuck was that He didn't like me), and the only way to earn His approval was adhere to the expectations of those "in authority".

Further complicating my experience was the disease of my family life. Both of my parents were raised in horribly dysfunctional families. The marriage of their mutual woundedness created a narcissist/enabler dynamic in which our family life revolved around the emotional status of the narcissist. From earliest memory, I became expert at perceiving unstated expectations, including the expectations contradicting spoken expectations, so that I could "be good enough to be loved." When I was four, our family left our home state to assist at a community farm that was part of our religious group, and thus began our trek away from extended family, getting farther away geographically and more distant emotionally from them. By the time I was 12, I barely knew anyone from extended family. My grandparents passed away as strangers. My cousins were unknown, other than as names. Aunts and uncles were vague characters in infrequently told stories.

We lived in several "community" situations and finally ended up in a rented house in a small northern community, which was the economic "source" for nine different community farms in our religious group. My family never lived in that home alone. We had a variety of people sharing our home—another family of six, a single mother and her daughter, a newlywed couple eventually joined by an infant, and a constant stream of single adults who would "come to town" over the winter months to earn money, which they then turned over to the leadership of their community. The message to me was that nothing, not even my parents, were "mine," and that to wish otherwise was sin. In other words, boundaries were sinful.

My most vivid memory from childhood was a keen awareness of the presence of the Divine. I remember as a toddler having conversations with God that were as real to me as my conversations with my parents, and in some ways more real, because I knew God understood me. As a toddler, I had no doubt I was acceptable to and loved by God. This assurance was eroded by outside messages so that by adolescence, I felt as if there were two Divine beings in my life. There was the private Divine, who was reassuring, comforting, and strengthening. Then there was the public Divine, who was disapproving and impossible to please, with hidden expectations. He sent Jesus to live the perfect life, which I somehow got to benefit from, but only if I lived as close to the perfect life as I possibly could.

In my early teens, my parents became disillusioned with this group and moved to a nearby town where we lived as a nuclear family for the first time since my preschool years. We attended an "established church" and discovered these "deceived" people actually had real relationships with God. But there were also hidden expectations here as well, reinforced by the expectations woven into my being from the womb. So while I heard far more often now that God loved me, I still felt the pressure of ever-lengthening lists of expectations. I received a lot of adult admiration for my "maturity" and "responsible behavior," which only intensified my sense of inner striving toward constantly changing goal posts of what a "Godly life" should look like. Woven throughout was the subtext of my parents' narcissism, which was its own source of changeable expectations and uncertainties.

But all of the double-speak felt normal. It never occurred to me there was any other way to exist or relate. Thus when I ended up at a fundamentalist Christian college in Texas at age of 17, the expectations and hidden messages fit right in with what I had known before. I experienced the first romantic attachment of my young life to a narcissistic young man whose dad was also narcissistic. I saw nothing wrong with the way they treated me or those around them. It was in that relationship reinforced by the religious setting that the erosion of my worth as female began its landslide.

At the end of my third year of college, I was given the shining gift of a nine-week student teaching assignment that took me to a tiny northern community. There I was gifted with nine weeks of spiritual and emotional intensive care. I lived with a dear Mennonite couple and worked in the church-school of which he was principal. This couple, as well as the church pastor and his wife, showed me unconditional love for the first time in my life. What I received there gave me the soul strength to finish my fourth year of college, as well as call an end to the emotionally abusive "romantic" relationship. I spent the next eight years trying to return to that place permanently. The two couples continued to support me long distance, and their loving care helped me get through the years that followed.

Cult Trauma

Cult trauma is a specific kind of religious trauma, even though it may have relationship with a variety of other kinds of religious trauma. Even though we might say there are elements of brainwashing in most systematized belief organizations whose aim is to bring power to few by diminishing or controlling the many, cult mentality is specifically highly focused on having no independent thinking of its members, It isolates the person(s) from any outside communities, especially family, and intentionally hones in on people's vulnerabilities to break them down.

While there are extreme versions of cults that can include things like mass suicide and mass sexual and physical abuses, there are also the subtler forms of cult behavior that may include many or most of the elements above but in a subtler fashion. As previously illustrated, there are yoga studios with power-driven leaders and self-help programs that might qualify as cult type in nature. The religious content and the doctrine and dogma (which usually reaches far from any traditional use or interpretation of the same texts) is singularly driven by enforcing control and serving power to a small number of leaders or a singular leader. Once someone is inside a cult community, it is very hard to extract him or her because if the brainwashing methods are effective, the person will not want or try to leave.

The symptoms of traumatic response post cult can be high anxiety, low self-worth and sense of identity, and guilt for leaving the community. Depending on the extent of abuse in the practices of the community, symptoms can include a variety of intrusive thoughts and nightmares, especially as the person begins to shed the brainwashing and see the practices of the community as dysfunctional and abusive.

LIFE PARABLE: Julie

My observations of the church led me to be even more suspicious of Christians than of other people. My dad was kicked out of his first church; it was a very difficult experience for my parents. I loved church because of my faith but was cautious. His third church and final year of pastoring left my mother in a state of complete mental breakdown, with three kids. A difficult situation in a small, private Christian school left me, at the age of 12, in a similar mental state. The only teacher of the small school didn't like me and made my life a living hell, and eventually I would have to be dragged into the school every day as I clung, crying, to the railing of the steps. Finally my parents took me out of the school after a meeting with the teacher and owners, who told my parents I needed to have a nervous breakdown because I was a perfectionist. After that I was terrified of school and authority figures and when we moved and started going to a large church, I was scared to participate in any of the youth meetings until I made a friend at school who started going with me. Later I went to Bible College where I met my husband, and he was a pastor for one year after graduation, so I was a pastor's wife briefly at the age of 20-21 in Canada, where I'm from. Shortly after we left that denomination, as we didn't agree with a lot of the doctrine, and through a series of events, we ended up moving to the United States and got involved with a different group of independent churches that described themselves as reformed charismatic. I would describe them as patriarchal puritans. I now call it a cult, and we spent about nine years there trying to be biblical. That was by far the most damaging church experience I had experienced as they focused almost solely on indwelling sin and how sinful we all are. Pastors had dictatorial authority over members, and men had the same kind of authority over their wives and children. We had three children while there, and I stayed at home where I belonged and asked myself many times a day as I had been taught, "What would my husband want?" It didn't work out very well, and after a difficult period of questioning, we decided to leave. I was very depressed and suicidal at that point, disdained all women, including myself, and thought I was absolutely worthless.

LIFE PARABLE: Gwen*

I am a woman who was raised in Bill Gothard's Advanced Training Institute (ATI) program.

Over the past two years as I have healed from the ravages of abuse, I have found power and healing in telling my story. I remember the first time I told someone I had been sexually abused. I stuttered over the words, cringing in shame and crushed by guilt. The more I tell my story and people witness the atrocities that happened to me, the more I have healed. Today I tell you my story without shame. I was very young when my parents first went to a Bill Gothard seminar. They sincerely believed his teachings were biblical and would "turn the heart of the parents to their children, and the hearts of the children to their parents" (Malachi 4:6). When I was going into second grade, Bill Gothard opened a pilot home school program, and my parents enrolled us as a second-year family. I was raised for 10 years in the ATI program, and it shaped every part of my being. As a child I was very fearful and craved security. Since that is exactly what the program offered, I embraced it wholeheartedly. I fully accepted every aspect of being under my authority's "umbrella of protection." I believed if I aligned even my desires (not just my actions) with the desires of my authorities, I would be the most happy. I remember one time a girl from my church made the comment, "Your parents are really strict!" I disagreed. I replied that actually they don't have "rules" for me. Instead they have trained my heart to want the very things they want for me, so I simply do what they expect without them having to tell me. This was something the ATI program taught parents to build into their children, and I was proud of the fact that I did it so well. As a result, my teen years were calm and peaceful. I never rebelled. It never even crossed my mind to think differently from my parents. If an authority wanted me to be a certain way, then that was God's best for me. By this time, I was completely unable to think independently or (God forbid) ever say "no" to an authority. If my authority's wishes were truly God's will for my life, why should I ever say no?

Ironically, this was exactly the outcome ATI was designed to create, and from the outside I was a complete success. However, in

*Extracted from a blog post on Recovering Grace, a forum for survivors of Gothard cult—with permission from author.

my heart all was not well. I began to live in daydreams and to feel horribly guilty about them. That was the beginning of the dichotomy between my tumultuous inside life and the perfect image I showed everyone on the outside. My family left ATI when I was nearing the end of high school. In the Baptist circles I grew up in, Bill Gothard was seen as too ecumenical. But as far as my life went, after college, the damage had already been done. I looked at all the stuff I was doing to be a successful Christian: daily devotions and prayer, proper dress and music, moral purity, work in the local church, evangelism, discipleship, and being a full-time missionary. But inside I was so desperately empty! Did God love me? Or even accept me?

After three months I was desperate for help but did not know how or who to ask. So I made a very loud cry for help: I overdosed on sleeping pills. My coworkers and mission board were shocked. My dichotomy was exposed. Everyone in my world could now see the truth about me: this "successful" Christian was really a great big *failure.*

But I saw hope from one source. My dad had a friend from college, and this friend had a daughter and son-in-law who ministered to broken Christians. Because they were family friends, I was happy to hear from them, and when they started emailing me, I was amazed. They helped me see that God loved and accepted me unconditionally. I was so desperate for this truth after my suicide attempt I decided to move back to the States and receive counseling from this couple.

The problem was that they were not Baptists, nor did they live a lifestyle separated from "the world," as I had been taught to live. All my authorities (my parents, pastor, Bible College) were adamant that I not go to this couple for counseling. They tried hard to warn me that I was too vulnerable and would compromise my higher standards by being around them. But for the first time in my life I had resonated with their message of unconditional love, so I disagreed with my authorities and directly "disobeyed" them. I was 25 years old.

I did not learn to think for myself overnight, however. While I soaked up my counselors' love and acceptance, trying hard to believe that God really loved me that way, I also became very codependent on them. I was trained to be dependent on others my entire life, and one solitary act of independence could not immediately change that.

…As it turned out, my counselor took full advantage of my trained submissiveness and began grooming me for sex. As my counselor, he controlled me emotionally, molding me to the place where I believed I could not survive without him. Over three long years he used my body. I would ask him to stop, but he said God was OK with it, and that when the time came, it would stop naturally. Over the years I was receiving "counseling" from this couple, I learned to self-injure, had multiple suicide attempts, ended up in a psychiatric unit four times, and developed an eating disorder. Finally, I had the courage to ask the counselor's wife for help, and I told her everything. She and her husband had a "reconciliation" meeting with me, in which we were each to apologize. However, they had my apology already decided. I was to ask them to forgive me for seducing him. I was stunned because I had no clue how I had seduced him. But being submissive, as I had been trained to do, I confessed to seduction. As a result, I believed I was a whore and an adulteress, and could never tell anyone my horrible secret. The sexual abuse stopped for a while, but because I never asked anyone on the outside for help, it eventually started all over again, and I still felt powerless to stop it.

Mercifully, God rescued me from the cycle of abuse. A man on their Board of Directors (who had been told of the abuse by the couple after our mutual apology session, but had been sworn to secrecy by them) suggested I move away. I had gone back to school since my return to the States and had become certified as a sign language interpreter, so for the first time in my life I actually had the means to be independent and self-supporting.

So at the age of 32, I began the journey to find a home and a job out of state. I was so excited that I actually had the ability to be independent! While Bill Gothard's ATI program seemed like a thing of the past for me, my parents still lived in that mindset and lifestyle. I remember the day my parents helped me move. We were up early to load everything and make the drive across the country to my new home. When we arrived, I excitedly showed them around, proud of my newfound independence. But my mom was horrified. She began to lecture me, saying I had done all of this outside of my father's authority, and wasn't I afraid of the judgment of God?

The next day as we were eating lunch, my mom tried again. She said, "Who you used to be is who you really are, and the way you are now is because you are deluded." It hurt deeply, but I was tasting freedom and wanted it too badly to give it up. With a great desire to heal, I found an eating disorder treatment hospital and made an appointment, as this had become a primary way my pain and suffering had manifested—in my body. I still believed that my counselor's sexual relationship with me was all my fault and that I had seduced him and was a whore. I felt intense shame. But that day in the nutritionist's office, I heard for the first time that what I experienced was sexual abuse, and that my counselor had violated professional ethics in using his position of authority to rape me.

After nine weeks of treatment in the hospital, I had the courage to tell my parents about my sexual abuse. They were heartbroken and very supportive of my healing. But after a few days, my mom asked me if I felt God's "conviction" against me for my sins. At first, I wasn't sure what she was talking about, but she explained. It was obvious to her that since I had chosen to go against all my authorities' wishes when I chose this counselor, I had sinned, and the sexual abuse was the natural consequence of that sin. I was crushed. Why, when I was already drowning in shame, did Gothard's principle of authority have to be used to pile on even more? It was this very principle that had held me hostage by causing an inability to say "no" strong or loud enough to those in authority abusing me.

Being in treatment gave me the strength to contact a couple of other members of the Board of Directors and tell them what my counselor had done. The text I received that day in June from my abuser was his last effort to get me to withdraw my accusations before the Board of Directors met. Thankfully, by then I had the skills to calm down and stand firm. In their meeting, the Board mandated that he stop counseling, and later that year they voted to close his nonprofit organization. More details have come out since, and I've learned I was not the only woman he abused.

Spiritual and Moral Injury Trauma

Spiritual and moral injury can be an included part of any of the above traumatic situations but also stands independently and may not always happen directly inside of religious contexts. As discussed earlier under the general categories of trauma, it is important to also list this kind of trauma here as it can occur in religious contexts or impact the spirit. This kind of injury comes from being engaged in practices, a situation, or community group that utilizes practices against a person's set of moral values. Sometimes the ability to see the difference of values may not appear immediately. Often after leaving religiously harmful communities, people begins to see more of the ways the systems beliefs do not match their own.

This process of realization can lead most prominently to feelings of guilt and shame, but also to issues of trust and intimacy with the self and others. The inner trust issues come from a realization that parts of the community or even one's own actions in the community were against their beliefs and morals—this can lead to guilt and shame that must be processed to be healed.

Other Related Religious Traumas

The traumatic experiences listed above are by no means a comprehensive list of all methods of traumatization in a religious context. This list is a way to begin a cultural and communal dialogue about how unhealthy, destructive, and abusive religions can hurt people and begin to validate those hurting experiences as traumas. My hope is that this list continues to expand and become more detailed as people feel more comfortable and safe to share their stories and journeys toward healing.

LIFE PARABLE: Deanna

I was in a theatre group in early high school that was my first exposure to good people who weren't also Christians. They were loving, warm, always excited when I was around, and wanted me for me, no strings attached. This was different than my faith community who expected me to dress a certain way, talk about Jesus a certain way, watch the right movies and listen to the right music, and have correct political opinions. I didn't realize just how much pressure there was until I was in a different environment. (I was an assistant director of a play, and at the time I knew I couldn't invite my friends because it had a few swear words, a kiss, and an allusion to sex. It was very lonely.) The second thing was that I ran into a guy from a community theatre production I had been in years before. He was my first love, with dark eyes, brown curls, and an infinitely young spirit. He wrote me letters and was always creating things by hand like leather-bound notebooks and silver rings. I was entranced. The only problem was that my church friends didn't like him. He made too many innuendos, swore occasionally, and I could never really verify if he was a Christian or not. But none of that mattered. I loved him. Between a bunch of theater nerds who loved me for who I was, and a love deemed unclean by my faith community at large, I started to see the cracks. How could these people who loved me and were there for me be the terrible people my church perceived them to be? Clearly, they were not.

As I mentioned earlier, I was hungry for more spiritual knowledge, so I went looking for it. I started going to the adult Sunday school classes instead of my own. I also wandered to other youth groups, groping for something more than what my church had been spoon-feeding me my entire life. Eventually the leadership got wind that I was exploring and trying other churches. The youth pastor called me one evening to find out what was going on, and when I told him, he proceeded to yell at me for 15 minutes. Every time I tried to interject to explain, he would talk over me. His wife did the same thing to me a few nights later, saying how her husband wasn't Billy Graham. All but one or two youth leaders abandoned me. When I shared my feelings with my church friends, many of them too deserted me. Another thing I noticed was their hypocrisy.

They preached all the time about love and looking out for the least, but they rarely ever did things with communities outside of the church body and missionaries. When a girl a few years older than I got pregnant out of wedlock, the church refused to host a baby shower for her because they "didn't want to condone her actions." She was left out in the cold.

They were strict about clothing for women too. One year they had a sexuality series in which the leaders said "ex" because they could not muster the strength to say "sex." They said that in the seven levels of physical contact, hugging was the closest thing to intercourse itself. There was a girl who was wear clothing that fit her nicely, and they deemed it immodest because it *might* come up when she bends over. So they had her change into the same outfit one size up, which looked frumpy on her, and they said this was the godly, modest thing to do.

They wouldn't let other students announce they were carpooling to Acquire the Fire event because elders at the church would frown on them promoting an event with rock music. These are just a few cases where I figured out the church was far more invested in control, piety, self-righteousness, and image than about the spiritual lives of their congregants.

CHAPTER 7

The Lotus and the Mud

The Sacred Wounds Healing Process

Where there is love there is life. —Mahatma Gandhi

There is a Buddhist philosophy based on the lotus and mud. The lotus flower is a beautiful and bright symbol of life, but the lotus grows out of the mud in swamps. There is no lotus without the mud—there is no joy without suffering; there is no transformation without grief. Buddhist images and metaphors of the mud and the lotus remind us that in the dankest, darkest, most messy places is born one of the most beautiful flowers on earth. Without the mud, we cannot create a lotus—nature, yet again, is the teacher of humanity. Without pain, there is no growth and transformation. We wouldn't seek out the mud, but we need it to grow. The healing journey looks like that—the blooming of a flower born from the dirtiest of places.

Hurt to Healing Explored

The following is a general outline of the process I went through in my faith hurt to healing trajectory. I would say much of life transformation and belief evolution moves in a similar pattern—although we may all have different side roads. A good portion of this book has included the stories, the "life parables" and anecdotes, which model the process of religious hurt and healing. We are still mining the hieroglyphics and ruins of these plundered and fallen castles of faith—as well as the restoration of the old structures or new buildings that make up the landscape of healing from religious hurt. Truthfully, before and after measurements and scientific methods, the data of our souls, wounds, and hope are always found in stories. Right now we are mining the information of the structures that will become tomorrow's scientific facts, measures, and methods. Join me as I delve into the stories of this particular nature of hurt and healing.

STEP ONE: Recognize the hurt, inconsistencies, or wrongdoing in your faith system—or with person[s] within your faith system. This process can take a minute or a lifetime depending on the circumstances.

STEP TWO: Begin to question. This can begin as an internal process. Depending on the strictness of your community group, it could be a completely secret endeavor or very public.

STEP THREE: Seek outside input. This may include seeking out a therapist or another kind of discernment professional. This might mean reading books or finding mentors who are asking the same questions you are and who are giving you the freedom to ask those questions and explore your ideas, belief, and feelings. This also might include finding Facebook or other online support groups of people seeking the same answers, or who are in different phases of their hurt and healing process in faith contexts.

STEP FOUR: Leave your spiritual home and/or faith of origin. This may also include leaving family, friends, and lifelong community members in the process. This phase is very emotional and includes many feelings of loss, confusion, and fear of the unknown on the other side of "knowing."

STEP FIVE: Begin your own pilgrimage into the spiritual desert—or as I called it, my spiritual runaway phase. This is the period where you begin to explore what your world, beliefs, and community context might look like without your faith of origin. This is a solitary journey.

STEP SIX: Enter the anger stage of grief and loss—which can also be accompanied with some kind of spiritual or philosophical nihilism. As you move away from the community that hurt you, like anyone who gets out of an unhealthy or abusive relationship and has time for the cloud of illusion to pass, you will most likely begin to get angry. Depending on the level of hurt you might often feel rage toward your own community group, but also toward any community—faith or otherwise. This can lead to a period of existential darkness or a kind of nihilism where it feels like nothing has meaning or value. In the extreme presentation of this phase, you can fall into a major depression or even begin to feel suicidal. While it is not essential to be in a religious tradition to find peace, we all need something in our life to have meaning and a way to understand the world to find happiness. Without this it is beyond lonely; it feels hopeless. This doesn't have to be forever, and if you are in this phase, know that it too will pass, If you are very depressed or suicidal, seek mental health counseling immediately.

STEP SEVEN: Explore other ideas, beliefs and opportunities. We can call this period religion shopping or maybe spirituality speed dating. This is a period that not everyone has, but many do. where people begin to explore other faith tradition. You may explore within other sects of your original tradition or within totally different traditions. A very common swap if you were hurt by a western faith tradition is to begin exploring eastern traditions because of their very different philosophies, faith languages, and practices. This also minimizes the chances for immediate triggers from your trauma—which would be harder to avoid if you stay in your own faith group.

STEP EIGHT: Begin to reintegrate meaning, values, and beliefs in some way for yourself—whether that is a mix of different ideas, philosophies and belief systems, or whether it is by joining a new community group or tradition. During this time you begin to understand yourself and your ideals better. There is more clarity to who you are as an independent person. Initially, because most people hurt by religion have felt stifled and without a voice, your initial set of beliefs may actually become a bit extreme in the opposite direction of your original faith, or even oppositional and defiant to these beliefs. Kind of like starting a new spiritual kindergarten, this is normal. Because you are usually fighting back and finding empowerment after being silenced, the initial response can be very absolute and black-and-white thinking. With time and experience this can soften—but it will take work. Just be forewarned, you have to do the work so you don't just become the staunchly oppositional version of where you came from or create a cycle of violence where you become the absolutist you left behind.

STEP NINE: Begin to trust in individual and communal relationships again. Once you have begun to integrate your belief system and start to know yourself better, you find that authentic relationships form organically from that place. You begin to understand that while everyone and every community is not trustworthy, it is worth the risk to try because we grow and heal in community (religious or otherwise) and in relationships (intimate and friendships). This may mean you are hurt, but it also means you are able to have amazing moments of collaboration and partnership with others that help make you stronger by supporting and championing your authentic self—just the way you are.

THE WILDCARD STEP: Anywhere along this process from hurt to healing, you can experience what I call the "wildcard." This is some hurt that comes and intrudes on your healing path and can either stall you or set you back again a few steps. If you know from the outset of this journey that the "wildcard" will happen—that we are all hurt again, that this is the inherent risk in trust, openness and authenticity—then you can prepare for it, expect it, and work to heal from it so it doesn't stagnate or permanently set back your healing process.

STEP TEN: Move toward a nondual consciousness or the middle way—and away from absolutes. The full integration of your healing process will come when you are able to see what the eastern traditions call the "middle way" or "nondual consciousness" and the western (and eastern) mystics find in their contemplative mindset. This usually requires some kind of contemplative practice to take us out of action and rightness and allow us to hold the tension between what we know, what we think we know, and what is "unknown." What this means is you no longer need to be right and can begin to understand that everything we can know from science or religion about the cosmos is a limited understanding of the ineffable. You can let go of black-and-white thinking, as well as what might remain of your hate and rage from your old wounds, and find a way to transform your hurt into healing action and good work for and in the world.

STEP ELEVEN: Enlightenment. Game Over. You Win! Ok, I am sort of kidding. But whatever comes after nondual consciousness might feel something like levitation—where gravity no longer applies to you. If you get anywhere close to step ten in a lifetime, be happy and know we all fall back sometimes into the earlier stages and places. We can't permanently exist in nondual consciousness. We just get morsels of its goodness before our ego gets back in the way or hurt tramples on us again, but it is the way we walk the path and not how far we get or how much we achieve that matters. Walk your journey with awareness, hope, and openness to what is possible, and you will land where you fit in the world and be authentically you when you get there. Healing from religious injury and spiritual abuse is a long and arduous journey. Honor every improvement and moment of healing you experience on the journey and all your efforts and hard work. You deserve a moment to honor yourself—even if you never levitate.

Now that I have set up a step process of the healing journey after religious trauma I want to explain how, even though I use the word steps, it is not a step-based system. Because we don't have very good language for a process of healing, growth, or transformation that moves deeper inward rather than upward, I am stuck with this upward language to describe an inward deepening process. To really get into the heart of a deepening process of healing transformation, I need to bring in a new, nondual concept of understanding healing, change, and growth.

While studying with Richard Rohr, a wisdom teacher in my life, at a place called The Center for Action and Contemplation, I was introduced to the theory of spiral dynamics and a phrase that could be the credo for life, "Transcend and include." This is more than a spiritual call. I think it is a healing necessity. When we have survived trauma, we know we can't just throw away experience—we can't eradicate memory or take away what has already happened. What we can do from a place of strength and empowerment is transcend and include.

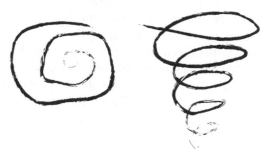

The images above symbolize a labyrinth and a spiral—which I am calling a healing spiral. If you look at it, though, it also could be just two different vantage points on the same symbol—one from above and one from the side. Both images illustrate an inward movement—on the left the labyrinth spiral moves inward; on the right the healing spiral move downward. This is the healing calling— to take with us what came before but not the emotional baggage attached, and to transcend—moving deeper and deeper to the root of our true and authentic self, carrying the wisdom, the heart and soul of our experience and what we have learned through healing, with us into our deeper levels of truth.

I say that simply, but not flippantly. This is not easy. To transcend, we must forgive and release hurt. To transcend, we must be able to let go enough to trust that our inward journey is taking us somewhere better—even and especially when it is uncomfortable to get there. That does not, however, mean we have to self-injure to heal. We have to take our time, and it may take some time. Transcendence of certain pains will take longer than others, but it is the pathway to healing.

While there is work to be done on the path from hurt to healing, I want to respect everyone's process in recovery from religious injury. In traumatic experience a person's choice is taken away. We don't choose to be hurt and often, especially in institutional settings, there is little empowerment and control in the hurt experience. I also want to articulate that the choice to heal—or how much to heal, when to stop on the path, and when to move forward—is everyone's to make. There is no right way or answer; there is only what is right for you. This is why I say regularly to my clients and when I am training providers: "Don't poke the trauma bear." What I is that the traumatic experience is painful and exposing as it is—there is no need to poke further into a person's pain or, if you are the survivor, to push yourself too hard too fast, or past your threshold for discomfort.

If you are trying to heal, or help walk through healing from religious trauma with others, you don't have to poke the trauma bear to get at the problem. You start with the first layer, the already exposed layer of trauma, triggers and symptoms already part of your present moment life experience. As you pull away the layers, or as you spiral inward, you go deeper into both the hurting experience but also into the healing and transformation of experience. Taking time in healing is critical. The process will go backward at points, and that is ok. All of our healing spiral journeys weave up and down—up to the surface and then down deeper—just like the rest of life experience. Take your process at your own speed, and if you are supporting someone in healing, let them make their choices of if and when to move forward on their healing journey. Choice is something we can take back after traumatic experience and something we deserve to own in our own lives.

LIFE PARABLES: The Healing Stories

ANONYMOUS: About four months ago, I commented to my husband that I felt I had discovered that the very bedrock of my life was turning out to be termite-laden, rotten wood. Thanks to his support, as well as the support and wisdom of my spiritual director, who also works in energy medicine, I've been able to face the layers of rubble, sit with the waves of pain, and begin to experience healing. I've discovered that what I thought was the foundation of my life was a façade, and beneath the facade is "What is real."

What is real?

Reality has turned out to be so much broader and more bountiful than I'd been led to believe. Because the tiny box of "acceptable spirituality" crumbled around me, I was able to see that the box itself was the problem, not all the "stuff outside" that I'd been told was so awful.

It's as though I was raised in a house of mirrors like one encounters at a carnival. That was all I knew, so I didn't know the images before me were distortions. I've been gently, yet inexorably, lured toward the Light. There are times I've felt blinded by that Light. The wide-open vistas have been nauseatingly disorienting at first. It's been terrifying at times to look at a world without reflective, distorting walls. But while I've suffered and wept, I've been held securely. The gift of awareness of the Divine that was with me as a toddler has never wavered. I've been supported, comforted, and given solace through the process.

My soul is still very tender. I have to take care whom I listen to and whose stories I let into my heart. It takes very little to overwhelm me … for the moment. A friend of mine had open heart surgery a couple of months ago, and it has taken time for his strength to return. I believe I'm on the recovery side of my "open soul" surgery, but I know healing continues to be a process and a journey.

My dream is to somehow, someday, be able to be a midwife others on their own healing journey. May it be so.

BILL: What I am clinging to is the idea that to see Jesus is to see what God is like, so I see this idea that Jesus is God incarnate. God moved into the neighborhood and showed us what God is like with the way he broke social norms and convention in his value of people. I extrapolate that this is what God's character is really like. To those who can't be in community, God says you are welcome and loved, and God will reach out and touch you. That is what is keeping me sane. I am still healing from a lot of hurtful and psychologically devastating images of God. I am concerned about how sectarian religion is; that whole us versus them binary. So one of the values is that religion can make you compassionate toward others, but in the United States it pushes you the other way. For me, I have the privilege of having access to technology that allows me to network and connect with people from different perspectives. I also have people in my life from communities I was once a part of, and a negotiation of relationship with people in communities I am no longer a part of is something that keeps me engaged outside of myself. One of the things I notice now, as someone in seminary, is that I never had any exposure to people of other religious traditions. I am 31 years old, and I just went to a Hindu temple and synagogue for the first time last weekend. As cosmopolitan as I like to think I am, I have not seen how these other traditions worship. A lot of my exposure to the world at large happens through social media and the Internet and listening to where other folks are, around what Phyllis Tickle calls "the Great Emergence." I think we are all in emergence because we are in cultural or societal upheaval—even if you are a staunch Baptist and thinking of how to go deeper in that you are still part of that swirl of change. Through blogging and reading different people, that is how I have begun to connect; we are all breathing the same air no matter where we are religiously and philosophically.

I think the best question I ever learned to ask is, "Why?" In my own healing, asking why a situation is affecting me the way it does and why I am doing what I am doing was important. We need to explore all that we do on the surface and the deeper dynamic it reflects. Coming in touch with our own trauma and hurt and not discounting things, we can only move past hurt in the greater context of understanding it—and we need to take trauma in religious context seriously. Things we have been taught about God can be really damaging. My spiritual journey is healing from trauma I have experienced in the church and my own life—I believe God wants to heal all things, and I can be a part of that story and experience that for myself. What do we think when we think about God? When those images are damaging, we need to take seriously those thoughts and community formed out of those negative thoughts and the trauma it can cause. We need to become serious about our healing from those things—not to discount it as not so bad or to just say we're going to move on without dealing with that trauma.

FAY: I have returned to the church several times, and I weep as I sing in worship because I deeply feel the words of the music and love music worship. But I am torn by the wonderful words and feelings and how different religion and the church really are from God. It is sad. I guess attending church is very connected with PTSD and the extreme feelings I experience when I attend. Maybe I will attend again in the future. I am a follower of the teaching of Jesus Christ, and I search for what that means in sorting out the religious corruption I have seen throughout my life. I want to live my life in a way that others are drawn to a relationship with Jesus Christ and God, so there is lots of love. I cherish the stories and the scripture recognizing that the Bible is to be understood in the context of how and why it was written. I pray and talk to God and question. I favor social justice, love, acceptance, and peaceful responses to anger and hate. I am remarried to a wonderful man who loves me unconditionally and has taught me so much. We are opposites. I am Protestant, and he is Catholic. We were both divorced but do not believe in divorce unless the marriage is abusive. (We were both abused in our relationships.) I am pacifist; he was in the military for 18 years. We love our children —my two daughters and his son—and we are a family committed to one another. We learn about God together, and we grow and change and heal. We are blessed to have found each other, but that is another story for another time. My spiritual journey is just that, a continuing journey. I miss the fellowship of others in the church and the community, and I support the memories of the good times that get mixed up in the memories of the trauma. Church picnics and always having a social place that was safe to see your friends can be a great social network for meeting others. I was privileged to grow up in a church where I heard the stories of the Bible and learned how much God loves us. Some people know nothing about God. That is sad. I would rather know about God and have some things that are messed up in the church's teaching then not to have been taught about Him at all.

HOPE: I believe that God is good all the time, . . .and that he allowed the crazy stuff to happen to us to help us grow into the people He wanted us to be. He took us to places in our spiritual and emotional development we probably never would have gone if we had a more peaceful life. It's also made us very passionate about healthy church life, justice, and churches not spiritually abusing.

DEB: Religion is not for me until I can find a denomination that fits with my personal belief system. I'm aware that my system may be wrong, but I'm sitting here writing about Him, and I would not have done that a few years ago. I believe we are called to love, take care, and treat one another as Jesus would treat us today. I have a lot to work on in the way of forgiveness, and I am not Christ-like in any way, shape, or form, but I am praying I continue my progress little by little. I speak of these things with my mother who has become my spiritual adviser, even though we don't always agree with each other, and I have deep conversations with my agnostic fiancé who was raised Episcopalian (quite different from Pentecostal and Baptist churches!) and my atheist friend. I have one other person in my life who has the same questions and who believes in Jesus, and it's very refreshing. It's hard for me to talk to any other members of my family. I read progressive Christian blogs and Facebook pages, but I don't have the guts to strike up conversations.

MARG: When AIDS first started killing people, Christians said some unbelievably awful things. It was clear to me that some Christians were responsible for delaying the research that might have been able to save gay men from dying. This changed me. I started hating Christians. I didn't hate people just because they said they were Christian, but I hated Christians in general. I avoided individuals who identified as Christian, because they would often say hurtful things or behave in thoughtless or exclusionary ways. I isolated from them, and I hated them as a group.

Almost all lesbians who were active in the lesbian culture were extremely anti-Christian. It's hard to describe, but to say that many of us felt about Christians the way Jews felt about Nazis would not be much of an overstatement. To this day, there are lesbian and gay people, most of whom are over 50, who still hate Christians and consider any LGBT person who identifies that way as delusional at best and a traitor at worst. But most LGBT people now know that some Christians are okay.

I got sober in the early 1990s when I was in my 30s. With my sobriety came clarity in the way I experienced the world. And with clarity came a longing for spiritual expression and experience. In the mid 1990s, I met some women who were Dianic Wiccans. This is a pagan, earth-based religion with a monotheistic, feminine divine presence (the Goddess), but also allows for an understanding that the divine presence is expressed in a great variety of female deities spanning cultures and ages. There is no eschatology and no one specific creation story. There is an emphasis on ritual, peacemaking, feminist activism, doing no harm, care of the earth, and surrendering oneself to the Goddess in love. I found the spiritual practice of Dianic Wicca quite appealing, and it was so different than Christianity that I was able to approach it without fear or trepidation. As a result, I became aware of myself as a spiritual person again and began to see myself in a similar way to how I had understood myself for the first 18 years of my life. It was as if I had been given back the key to my soul.

A few years after that, I sat in on a workshop presented by a therapist named Katherine Unthank. A psychologist, a born-again Christian, and a lesbian, she had a similar experience to mine, having found herself unwelcome in her own church after coming out. As a therapist, she was able to recognize what happened to her during and after this experience as trauma. She had developed a theory that what the church did to LGBT people was best understood as a form of spiritual power rape, and what happened to the LGBT people as a result had much in common with the PTSD experience of women who have been physically raped. She detailed symptoms one might develop after this experience, and in doing so, described the last 15 years of my life. I sat stunned, hardly able to breathe or move, and for the first time I began to understand what I had lost when I told the youth minister I was gay. I had lost everything I knew or thought my life would be, the legacy of my grandmother and my mother, and the only safe place I had.

As the numbness of 15 years started to wear off, I began to cry. For years I had hardly even let a tear run down my cheek, but now I cried for two days straight. Sobbing. Realizing, for the first time what had been unfairly taken, just because I happened to be a lesbian. Over time I worked through my grief. Fortunately I found a therapist who recognized the depth of this loss and helped me come to terms with it. I still didn't like Christianity, and I stayed afraid of Christians. But I began to heal. In 2002, by chance, I ended up being hired to do sound for a group called the Evangelical and Ecumenical Women's Caucus. They were holding their conference in Indianapolis. I'm still a little shocked I took the gig, but I needed the money and figured I could lay low and live through a weekend with a bunch of church ladies.

I was shocked when I discovered these women turned out to be no ordinary church ladies. EEWC was a gender justice organization that had voted to support LGBT equality way back in 1986. Their founding members included Letha Dawson Scanzoni and Virginia Ramey Mollenkott, authors of one of the first books to make a biblical case supporting inclusion and welcome of LGBT people in Christianity, *Is the Homosexual My Neighbor?*

I spent that weekend watching and interacting with a group of feminist Christians, learning, worshipping, and sharing fellowship with one another. The lectures were the most stimulating I'd experienced since leaving school. Talking with lesbian Christian feminists was mind blowing. The last day there was a worship service. It was the first Christian worship service I had attended in years, and it affected me deeply. I sat at the soundboard, trying to do my job while holding back giant waves of emotion. I was taken back to the first 18 years of my life, when this had been my weekly reality. I remembered how it felt. I cried, tried not to sob, and hoped no one was noticing. The women got up and moved forward to take communion. One of the founders of the organization, Nancy Hardesty, saw me sitting in the back and noticed my tears. I think she knew exactly what I was feeling. As I tried to stop crying and become invisible, she casually walked right up to me, leaned over, and whispered in my ear, "You are always welcome at Her table." Then she turned and walked back to her seat. I didn't know what to think or feel. As I worked that afternoon, tearing down the system, I tried to talk to my partner about what had happened. But she couldn't understand, or I couldn't explain it. I tucked that weekend away, but kept it close to my heart.

Four years later, the Indiana chapter of the organization called me out of the blue to see if I wanted to come to a meeting. I said yes, and thus began my involvement with EEWC. Thus began my journey back to Christianity. I have been active with EEWC ever since, becoming their office manager and web developer in 2012 and their director of public information in 2013. It didn't matter to them that I wasn't able to refer to myself as a Christian. I think they know my heart better than I did. For a very long time, saying I was a Christian felt like taking on the label of my perpetrator. I don't know what changed this year. I don't know why I started to be able to say it, but I think maybe it was that I stopped being afraid that some of my LGBT friends would hate me. Christian is still a dirty word to some LGBT people because their wounds have never healed. I never let go of Jesus, but as long as I was afraid of those claiming to be His people ,there was a separation.

I don't have a church anymore, and I don't think I ever will again. I'm still too triggered by being around groups of people and by the way church people often act. I'm hypervigilant and always looking for the judgment and exclusion to show itself. I can't imagine a time when I will feel safe in a church. But I have found my people, my tribe, and my faith community in the women and men of EEWC-Christian Feminism Today. They are my friends and mentors. They are my mothers, sisters, and brothers. And I am beginning to realize my heart is safe with them.

EMMA: I see a lot of healing on the brink right now, even the work I see my sister doing to push more intergenerational trauma and healing issues forward and get people trained to understand intergenerational/historical trauma. As they learn more about themselves and that they are healing themselves, they can see the trauma others are going through too. A lot of times I felt really alone—it comes from my abandonment issues—and so I have to do self-talk to pull myself out of that. When I get a trigger, I can see where the trigger is coming from and talk myself out of it.

For me spirituality is so huge in the work that I do that I don't know how to help people heal if they aren't connected with any sort of spirituality. I ask people I work with, "What do you believe in?" I always tell them that due to the way I grew up, I learned it is ok to believe in *all* ways (for me that includes Native and Christian spirituality), and I help them heal by calling their spirit back.

I see a lot of the healing work starting now because there is so much awareness around the intergenerational trauma issue in and out of faith communities. Currently there is more awareness of Native American people. We felt invisible, and society treated us that way. Now people are getting their voice and seeing how they can move toward healing. With social media, there are people who can see they are not alone and are learning about intergenerational trauma in social media forum.

The people in social services and support programs are starting to come now on the reservations, and they weren't before. Right now my coworker and I from the White Bison Mending Broken Hearts program (healing program for intergenerational trauma) are working with Bishop John in the Episcopal Diocese of South Dakota to bring two more of our healing programs to South Dakota and the Lakota people who live there. Bishop John truly cares about helping people, and for me that is so heartwarming because I didn't feel that way growing up from my church community. He understands about the intergenerational trauma and how important it is to do this work.

For me, to see that in South Dakota is unbelievable, to see there is this bishop who cares. My hope is I can help people to discard their old beliefs, hurts, and traumas instead of setting up blocks. When I moved toward healing, I had to let go of a lot of my old negative beliefs. My hope moving forward is that there can be many more programs like the ones we are working on now. I hope the church could work with the community to help it heal.

KISHA: At this time, I am not solid in my theology at all. I try to remain open. I believe there is a God simply because I believe it was Him who transcended and transformed my darkness on the day that would have been the last day of my life. No one else was present. No one else helped me. No one else could even reach me. It was just me, my darkness, and my plans to end it all until I experienced this luminous disruption. However, in spite of my belief in God and in Christ, I am very leery of Christian/Church culture. In my heart of hearts, I am not at all interested in church, though I am interested in community. However, I am very concerned about the hearts and souls who sit on church pews Sunday after Sunday, week after week, and get hurt, abused, mislead, and misinformed. If we are going to have church, I would rather take the lead so I can know people are being cared for well, however, I keep running into the same problem I had as a child: I don't fit into the church system, and I continue to be rejected. For some reason, I am a threat to the current equilibrium established within most church systems, therefore, the easiest thing to do is dismiss me, silence me, and push me out.

As a chaplain I will have an alternative route for which I can care for people spiritually. Instead of being pressured to be "on" all the time, or to conform to the bullshit laced within church culture, I can merely go straight to the source, meet people where they are, and be a present help in the midst of their darkness. That is what I am excited about—presence, not performance.

In the meantime, I practice community with the local spoken word and open microphone artists in my area. I have learned there are some very common threads that run deep among poets, prophets, and preachers. Therefore, I make it my business to commune with such folks at least once or twice weekly. My loyalty to church attendance is not as significant. However, when there is something of interest happening at church, such as a book study I'm interested in, I attend. The United Methodist Church denomination seems to be a safe space for me during this particular season of my life.

Rage and Reconciliation: Reconciling on the Healing Journey

Martin Luther King, Jr., once said, "Hate cannot drive out hate, only love can do that." This quote has been repeated over and over, yet our personal and cultural history seems to reflect hate trying to beget love, freedom, and hope. It never can, and it never has. This does not mean we obliterate necessary justice, but it means that for it to have any transformative power, that justice must be wrapped in inner and outer movements of reconciliation. Without reconciliation, rage is just the leftover matter of hate and abuse. We cannot create a life on just the hate of the wrong; we must build on the praxis of the good.

As a trauma therapist and survivor, I have personally and professionally spent much of my life mired in the sewage of abuses. This, however, is not the only thing that can come from trauma—we all have the potential to transform hate into love. Many times, though, we get stuck in the sludge of the hurt and get so entrenched that we can't find our way out to healing.

I run an intensive outpatient and outpatient program in Southeast Florida for survivors of trauma and addiction. In the program are three things I have found inherent to healing: creative expression, spiritual and embodied practices, and relational experience. To articulate the depths of sewage we can get mired in, I show my clients a clip from *Shawshank Redemption*. This is one of my all-time favorite movies.

The anthropologist, philosopher, and decipher of myths Joseph Campbell would say it is because the story speaks not just to the story of one man, but because to every man and woman—illuminating the inherent struggle of humanity. Joseph Campbell believed that all stories, be they religious parables or contemporary cinema, tell all our stories over and over. He calls this "the hero's journey." When I see *Shawshank Redemption,* I am reminded of this hero's journey, and this is why I share it with all of my clients.

The clip I show is near the end of the movie when the protagonist, Andy Dufresne, frees himself from the prison of his own rage, resentment, and guilt by chipping away, year after year, at the concrete walls of his cell until he reaches the path out. Andy's friend "Red" narrates his escape path, saying, "Andy crawled to freedom through 500 yards of shit smelling foulness I can't even imagine, or maybe I just don't want to. Five hundred yards. That's the length of five football fields, just shy of half a mile." The scene ends with him exiting the tunnel of crap, stripping bare his prison clothes, and standing in the midst of rain and lightning with his hands spread wide as he looked up to the sky, into the heavens.

The reason I show this clip is because the road out of trauma and suffering is like the miles of waste that Andy Dufresne crawled through. The question of our lives is: Are we willing to crawl out of the crap and into freedom, or do we sit in the sludge or behind the prison walls of our pain forever? This is where the choice comes in. This is where we decide who we are in the mythology of our own lives.

Interestingly, the film is an adaptation of a novella written by Stephen King titled *Rita Hayworth and Shawshank Redemption.* I say "interesting" because Stephen King was a survivor of childhood trauma, which I learned in graduate school when reading a book by psychiatrist Lenore Terr about the impact of childhood trauma on the life and personal mythology of those who survive terrible things in their early lives. Much like Joseph Campbell, although she doesn't use the same language set, Terr believes we tell the stories of our pain in our lives, and our myths will follow us. She explored the relationship between Stephen King's own childhood trauma and his experience of writing stories of horror (and sometimes healing). To me, *Shawshank Redemption* is one of King's best stories of surmounting the horror to find freedom.

In the film, after Red recounts this story of escape from suffering, he closes by saying, "I remember thinking it would take a man six hundred years to tunnel under the wall with it [an old rock hammer]. Old Andy did it in less than twenty…Andy Dufresne, who crawled through a river of shit and came out clean on the other side."

We all have this potential. This is why I remind my clients of this story. We all have the ability to move through the crap of our suffering and come out clean on the other side. Or we can sit in rage and hate. Both are choices. We decide which way we go, but transformation is only available to those who crawl through the crap. We cannot control who hurts us, in and out of faith, but we can control how we respond. I have seen so many people live their lives in the tunnel of bile and sludge, and many who live inside the prison forever.

We cannot control what happens to us, but we can control what we do with it.

Reconciliation in Healing, Healing in Reconciliation: Lessons from the Reservation

I have worked on internal and personal reconciliation out of trauma and hurt with clients for years, but I think I have learned the most about the path of reconciliation both personally and communally from my work with indigenous communities and the Doctrine of Discovery with colleagues from the Episcopal Church. The profundity of reconciliation with Native peoples and Christianity cannot be underplayed. To be a Native person and a Christian, or even to live in contemporary Western culture in and of itself requires an inherent dimension of reconciliation and forgiveness. Two parts of a person are torn between loving and living in the communities who hurt their families and ancestors and many times even those in their present-day lives.

I have learned a few lessons of the tether-holding healing and reconciliation together—as two essential pieces of the same process.

1. **Healing and reconciliation are bound together.** To have whole person healing, you need to find a way to reconcile the hurts of the past. This does not mean to forget it or ignore the wrong, or avoid seeking justice, but to internally find a way to heal from the hurts others have imposed on our lives. —Otherwise, this power

of the trauma and the abuser will always have more control over our lives than we do.

2. **No one is mandated to heal—it is a choice.** We have to respect that choice when it is made by others, and we have to be tender with ourselves if we are not ready to find internal reconciliation for our wounded experience.

3. **The healing and reconciliation path continues communally, even if some are not ready to make the journey.** It's like going to a big event—not everyone fits on the first shuttle, and not everyone is ready to get on, but the shuttle bus leaves with whoever gets on board, and then comes back around until everyone who wants to get to the event has a chance to get on board. But the event doesn't wait to start until everyone gets there—we just get on at different points and get to the healing and reconciliation process in our own time.

4. **Until we have found our own way to reconcile our hurts and let go of hatred and rage, we will carry that heavy part of our wound with us.** There are amazing methods for creating safe space and communal dialogue about communal hurts I have come to know from Native communities doing this work. Their models lend us a lot of good source material for how we can create the communal healing, as well as the individual healing.

5. **Education and justice are just as important as healing.** To have people understand this hurt experience and to have a safe space where people can tell their stories and ways to organize around transformation justice are essential. But without the healing and inner reconciliation, the external healing and engagement with a communal process is not yet possible.

6. **Heal in your own time and find your own path to inner peace.** There will always be another shuttle bus whenever you are ready. We must honor our own journey, and our own journey needs to be honored by others.

As trauma healing from religious injury becomes more talked about, and formulas for both individual and communal reconciliation and healing are begun, there are many things we can learn from our Native brothers and sisters on how to manifest this process powerfully and respectfully for all involved. They have been holding the tension between healing and reconciliation, as well as trauma and faith, for a very long time.

CHAPTER 8

Just for Today

The 12 Steps, Community, and Recovery from Religious Injury and Spiritual Abuse

The wound is the place where the Light enters you. —RUMI

In the fall of 2009, I moved from New Jersey to Southeast Florida. I had just gotten married the previous New Year's Eve and my husband, Chris, and I had both become tired of long, hard winters, ice scrapers at 6 a.m., and the New York City Metro area five-mile and 45-minute commute. I had previously lived in Colorado, and ever since, I had been aching for a slower and quieter pace of life. Even though my time in Colorado was colored by the fact that I had been dealing with PTSD run wild—post-trauma having fled to the mountains to ease my own traumatic pain—I always told myself that if I had lived in the Rockies in a less chaotic time of life, I would never have left. Chris was feeling drawn to return to Florida, where he had spent the happier part of his life, in the safe space of his grandparents' home in Boca Raton. He often spoke nostalgically about his summers at the beach, a thousand miles away from the fighting of his soon-to-divorce parents, and the addiction and mental health issues that swarmed around his growing up experience.

We were in a place in our personal, relational, and professional lives where we had licked our own past wounds and found healing and recovery from our pasts—in a good portion if not entirely—and had both joined the counseling profession. I was a trauma therapist at the Department of VA for combat veterans and survivors of military sexual trauma, and he was working for the prison system in an addiction and rehabilitation program for soon-to-exit inmates. We felt driven and passionate about our work, but essentially wanted to do it somewhere with a little more sunshine and summertime, if possible.

We landed in Delray Beach, Florida, totally unknowing it was probably exactly the spot in the universe for a trauma therapist and addiction therapist couple to land. Addiction recovery, with the same motivation toward sunshine and summertime, moved to Delray a couple of decades previously and created a large network of treatment centers, halfway houses, and a lively addiction recovery community like nothing I had ever seen before. Instead of one meeting in a church basement once a week, in Delray there was a meeting every hour, on the hour, if you were in the market for it. In truth, besides clients I worked with, until that point I had very little interaction with recovery as a community dynamic. It was one of the greatest gifts to be immersed in. Of course like any group with tenets and doctrine, there are the fundamentalists in recovery, but what I found even more than that was a caretaking community of people in their 20s and 30s, people who would have been anomalous and possibly outcasts in their home cities across the country where a 20-something who doesn't have a glass of wine or cocktail on a Friday night is looked at as strange, even unwelcome. However, here in Southeast Florida, people were willing to help their neighbors and even strangers, held no judgment for people's past life errors, pains, or hurts, and offered unconditional acceptance. In many ways, it mirrored for me everything I hoped for religion on its best of days. Much like a system of belief, of course, there were the zealots, egomaniacs, fundamentalists, and condescending personalities. However, the system and doctrine as a whole offered something powerful that I wanted access to in general. In Delray, unlike anywhere else I have known, if you meet someone and they are not in recovery, it is kind of unusual.

I felt blessed to have a lens into this private tribe and subculture with principles that had so much to offer for so many. My husband and I started a young adult spiritual seekers group, which was near the downtown area, and so many of our attendees were in early recovery. A spiritual community built up out of the principles these people lived by—informed by it in their actions, not by any doctrine they espoused. They just acted based off of the principles they had learned in their healing and recovery. They were open, inclusive, and communal, and I deeply believe the spiritual community we have today is just as much so, because of the principles they offer to our space and the Christian content we offer to theirs. It was definitely mutually beneficial. We wanted to create a safe space for people to seek, ask questions, and learn about the good stuff Christian tradition had to offer—a respite for those religiously wounded and a starting point for those wanting some kind of spiritual community but not knowing where to start.

That said, like all cultural outsiders (as described in the negation categories of church-hurt), people in and out of faith culture still have stereotypes, stigmas, and negative beliefs about people groups. Although I have become more adept at living the tension of being on the fringe of faith culture—in it enough to hopefully be useful, but out of it enough to not be constantly brokenhearted—there are moments of triggering that sometimes I still can't breathe through. One of those moments came when a member of my home-base church said recently to my husband, after almost 20 people in our community engaged in baptism as a symbolic connection to their spiritual journey, "Well, they don't count. I mean they're not really part of the church. They're all addicts." Yep. This happened. So, sadly, yet again, those people who don't get it are still going to not get it. But I try not to spend my time with that. It is also why those people who separate, segregate, and prejudge or categorize others don't get the benefit of seeing the sacredness of all paths—and the benefits of connection and communication with other people's journeys.

When we do faith and spirituality well, and share the riches, we can be exposed to systems and communities that have much to offer us. The 12 steps is one of those gems I was gifted with and for which I am forever grateful. Plus, I have gotten used to being the one "normie" (aka not in recovery) person in my usual crowd of friends, although, as I have learned from studying the steps, we are all in recovery from something—especially those of us healing from trauma and emotional wounds. It is a tool I think we can all benefit from, so I want to share a trauma-conscious, spiritual wounds approach to the 12 steps as another tool you may choose to use on your healing journey.

A 12-Step Path

The following is a breakdown of the 12 steps as it can aid all of us in hurt and healing, helping anyone who has been hurt by life, faith, or religion to find a whole, person-centered recovery process. We could all benefit from a whole person and society review of the 12 steps and what, in its healthiest manifestation, it has to offer all humans and especially those seeking healing from traumatic experience.

As I will repeat, especially on some of the harder steps, don't walk this path alone. In the traditional recovery model, this process is meant to happen in community and, at the very least, in partnership with another. This is for both support and accountability. To be this vulnerable, we need to have someone who says it is ok to do so and will hold safe space and unconditional love for us through the process. If you have a group or community you have been sharing your hurting journey with—other survivors—you might want to walk the step together. If you have a mentor, therapist, or life partner, you might want to walk with them through these steps as a support. If you are in traditional addiction recovery, or recovery for codependency, an eating disorder, or sex addiction, or else in another 12-step program, you might want to move through these trauma-conscious steps for faith hurt with your existing sponsor or a new sponsor who might be better suited for this process. If you are in some kind of spiritual discernment or guidance, or are working with a spiritual director, you could work with that person through the 12 steps. You just want to not work through this process or any facet of the healing process alone. There are safe places and people—find them where they are in your world and walk with them for support and companionship on the journey.

12 Steps for the Religious Injury and Spiritual Trauma Experience

1. **We admit we are being hurt by our human addictive nature (as it is manifesting as addictive compulsive response to others and as our hurt and anger, and to unhealthy systems/ communities/leaders, etc.). We admit our lives have become controlled by whatever we are addictively holding onto.** We all have inherent addiction and compulsions we follow—often to stop hurt; sometimes to numb out enough just to survive

another day. I often say that smoking is a breathing exercise with consequences. Traumatic response is like that—whether we self-medicate with drugs or alcohol, with emotional numbing or dissociation, or with panic attacks or rage—they are all coping skills with consequences. We become addicted to our feelings, hurt, and response to traumatic experience, and sometimes we are still nursing addiction and the suffering of a system/leader who had us rely on them as a the living tools of how to cope or live in life. Sometimes the system we were in is the addiction we are trying to kick. Whatever it is—the addiction is just our human ego trying to find a place to act out its neurosis or narcissism. There is something or some things in our way that we need to let go of—find what those are for you. See what it feels like to stop trying to get rid of it alone. As a good friend of mine regularly says, "We are wounded in isolation; we heal in community." First we give over our will that we can control everything ourselves, and then we grow in a healthy version of community and/or mentorship to find a healthier way to live.

2. **Come to believe that a power outside of ourselves (God, the universe, the cosmos, that which can transform me) could restore us to wholeness and health.** Whatever it is that is greater than our own fear, anxiety, anger, or ambition can help us heal—this may be moral, religious, or philosophical for you. This could be something offered to you from a wisdom teacher or close friend—something greater than what you know in this moment is the guidepost to your growth and transformation. When we believe we are the ultimate source of all our answers, even if out of fear, we can become like the institutions or false gurus of certitude we left behind. To avoid that, we all have to find reference points greater than us, and what we know today, to guide us forward. Consider who, what, and where you can find those in your own current life.

3. **Make a decision to seek safe space, acceptance, and guidance from the power outside of ourselves (God, the universe, the cosmos, that which can transform me), and that which manifests as this Power in the world (wisdom teachers, communities, helping professionals, and texts that expand our awareness of self and others, and help us find safety and healing).** Especially in early healing and recovery, even more

so if we have been hurt by other people or people groups, our process of licking our wounds becomes private, which can also lead to feelings of pain, guilt, depression, sadness, grief, loss, and anger, which just stir inside ourselves without any external outlet or resources to help us through the pain. Finding a safe space or spaces with others, master teachers, or therapists or trusted friends, who can help us see outside of the pain and find the beginning path to healing, is essential. Find that which feeds and provides you unconditonal love and acceptance, and nurture yourself while you heal inside of that space[s].

4. **Make a searching and fearless moral inventory of ourselves to see unhealthy actions, patterns, and behaviors and how they manifest in our own lives—so that we are not doomed to repeat them.** In the early stages, the impetus can be to close up internally as a self-protection mechanism and to not see outside of the pain of having been hurt. This can become overwhelming and doesn't help us move forward on our own path toward healing, wholeness, and discovering our truest and most authentic self. Part of transformation is also introspection to see our own unhealthy patterns—often built out of the trauma experience, what an abuser might have said or imposed, and whatever protective mechanisms we created that are no longer serving us. Seeing ourselves clearly and honestly is a key part to our own healing, growth, and development.

5. **Admit to the power outside of ourselves (God, the universe, the cosmos, that which can transform me), to ourselves, and to another human being the exact nature of our hurt, broken places, trauma, regret, and moral indiscretions of the past, and how that has impacted ourselves and others in our lives.** This part can include telling our stories, but it is also more than just telling—it is telling in a way that is vulnerable, honest, humble, and transparent about our journey and hurting places in our life. It also means we have to see how our pain journey has impacted others and ourselves. Part of any process of transformation, like the 12 steps and this version created around the specific issues of religious injury and trauma, is taking things at your own pace. This step (as all) brings its own sense of difficulty. Be kind to yourself. If you are not ready to go there, hold off. The greatest benefit of this process is that it

is meant to be personal but also communal. Share the journey with someone—a therapist, teacher, or confidant. You don't have to walk into these difficult places alone.

6. **Become open to transforming ourselves with the help of the Power outside of ourselves (God, the universe, the cosmos, that which can transform me), and be willing to do the work to let go of whatever we are holding onto from our past that is holding us back or inside our pain and pain experience.** This step is a preparation for the work of the steps that follow. We have to be ready and willing in some respect to heal and let go of what is still hurting us about our past. That doesn't mean forgetting. That doesn't mean not speaking out. That doesn't mean not seeking justice. It just means that transformative speak, actions, justice, and living can be most beneficial from a healed and transformed heart. This means you have to be willing to do the work to let go of the pain, suffering, and anger of your past hurt to do better in your life for yourselves and others. It will happen in bits and pieces, not all at once. Like a snake shedding skin, you have to be willing to work to make that process happen and be open to it, one step at a time.

7. **With the support of others, our own intention, and the Power outside of ourselves (God, the universe, the cosmos, that which can transform me), work to remove those things (listed earlier) that haven't served us, our lives, or others from our minds, hearts, and spirits—and remove the heaviness on our conscience about these issues. We give ourselves permission to forgive ourselves for anything we are holding onto about ourselves, and our actions.** This is the next layer of willingness and preparation—we must prepare our heart, mind, and spirit to let go of that which isn't serving us from our past behaviors and feelings—and we begin to prepare ourselves to be able to offer forgiveness for the wrongs done to us—more for our benefit and healing than anything else. To be unforgiving is a heavy load to carry.

8. **Make a list of all persons we had harmed and become willing to make amends to them all. Make a list of all persons who have harmed us and become willing to offer forgiveness to them.** This is just writing the list—which can be taxing but it is preparation or offering the amends to people or, if you choose,

forgiveness to others. Write the lists honestly and authentically—
and be gentle with yourself in the process.

9. **Make direct amends to such people whenever possible, except
when to do so would injure them or others (or us in context to
our healing at this moment in time—we can always return to
amend later if it is currently not emotionally safe to address
it in the present). Make a conscious effort to forgive those
persons, communities, or institutions that are holding onto
hate and unforgiveness—this does not mean they are not
culpable; it just means we won't carry around the burden of
their wrong deeds on our mind, heart, and spirit.** This is a
very difficult thing on both ends. It may take time, and some
on both lists may take time to address. With trauma, especially
hurtful community trauma, this may or may not include an
actual formal forgiveness to others—for some people that serves
a purpose or a public catharsis. For others, the forgiveness will
be private and personal and may just happen in their heart.
Sometimes it might include writing a letter that is never mailed
to the person[s] you want to forgive. The forgiveness you get
unburdens your heart; the forgiveness you give does the same—
regret and unforgiveness are heavy burdens to carry, and one
of the hardest ingredients of whole person healing is the inner
process of reconciliation.

10. **Continue to be aware of our actions and motives, and work
to remove those things that hurt ourselves or others and are
not serving us when we act from an unhealthy, rageful, or
wounded place. We will also admit when we have acted from
those places to keep ourselves honest and transparent about
what we do and why we do it.** To continue on the healing path,
stay humble, and grow and transform, we have to be honest
and authentic with others and with ourselves. If we don't, our
process of healing and growth can stagnate, and we can become
entrenched in one way of thinking about ourselves and acting in
the world. Constant review of ourselves, patterns, and behaviors
is vital to a full and whole life in healing and in general.

11. **Practice contemplative methods and practices (mindfulness,
meditation, contemplative prayer, etc.) to improve our
awareness, consciousness, healing, and transformation as well
as to connect with the Power outside of ourselves, whatever**

we call it (God, the universe, the cosmos, that which can transform me). Engage in these practices to increase insight and connect with our true and authentic self—so that we might continue to act out of that authentic place and not out of our hurts or anger. Contemplative practice and mind are an essential piece of a balanced life. That is why this practice was in the 12-step traditions from the start, why the contemplatives and mystics from every religious tradition around the world (and their most healing manifestation of religion) include long lineages of contemplative practice, and why even the contemporary mental health community is integrating mindfulness and contemplation to the treatment of everything from depression to anxiety to PTSD. Whatever way you practice contemplation in your life is up to you—it can be in breathing exercises, mindful nature walks, contemplative prayer, or Eastern meditation practices. Find the contemplative path that best fits you and your life, and engage with it deeply and regularly. It is a critical dimension to authenticity, transparency, and transformative healing.

12. **Having achieved spiritual insight and awakening, or some form of personal transformation as a result of these steps, we practice offering the message and practice of these steps to others healing from hurt and seeking personal transformation out of their own addiction (to self, others, hurt, unhealthy systems or feelings, etc.). We continue to practice the principles of these steps in our daily life—building and growing our insight and becoming aware and connected with our authentic self as we move deeper into our healing.** We are most whole when we can take what we have received and give it away, in some fashion. Share these principles, your journey, and others' healing path. Help others along the way with what you have learned so far—you would be amazed how much you can help. You are valuable, and your help is needed from someone else walking your same path. Reach out, build community, and be honest and vulnerable enough to help others in community and in companionship.

Despite some ignorance still about recovery—as exemplified by the woman in my home community—there is great wisdom in these principles, and I have seen lives riddled by addiction and trauma transformed by their content. Like anything, it can't be the "be-all, end-all" only method on your healing journey. As we transform, we need a variety of things to meet us at each step of the road, but these methods can be great tools for self-discovery when integrated into a healthy healing and recovery path. You can also explore other methods of recovery online—there are meetings all across the country for an increasingly varied number of 12-step programs. The world may be catching up to the inherent truth that if we have an ego, and we all do, then we can be compulsive. Heroin may be an obvious addiction or compulsion, but addiction to power is no less addictive and potentially as destructive. If we can see ourselves as inherently equal to all, then we can see our own human issues as no less problematic or in need of recovery as the person whose addiction stands out as largely as heroin. Use these steps above as you will, if they are useful on your healing path.

CHAPTER 9

The Voices Out of Darkness

Messages from Survivors to Survivors and Faith Communities

He who sees all beings in his Self and his Self in all beings, he never suffers; because when he sees all creatures within his true Self, then jealousy, grief, and hatred vanish. —THE UPANISHADS

The voices of hurt and healing are powerful. This is the reason that woven throughout this book are the voices of those hurt and of some who have found healing on the other side of religious injury. I can think of no more effective way to provide support for those suffering from this kind of traumatic experience or anyone else more equipped to speak to those in faith traditions. This does not necessarily mean faith traditions with overt injury to their community members but includes those who wish to do faith better and serve those who have been wounded, rather than discount them as frivolous, superficial, or without deep spirituality. As much as I have met those who have left faith traditions seeking the solace of other voices, I have also met those inside traditions trying to create a safe and healthy community but who don't have the tools to know how to provide a nurturing environment for wounded souls and hurt hearts. This section of the book speaks out loud from the voices of those who have been wounded to those who are suffering sacred wounds. Then, in turn, it speaks to those in faith communities wishing to understand and

155

nurture those who have been hurt, and who ardently want to do faith better and support those healing. This chapter is for both ends of the spectrum—written by the voices who from experience know the arduous and painful journey, as well as the potential for hope and healing.

TO SURVIVORS...

THE QUESTION ASKED: *What do you wish people who are being hurt by their faith communities could know?*

HOPE: What I would like to tell people currently being hurt by their faith communities is two things: 1). God sees and knows, and *he will* avenge the wrong things done to them in His time. The truth will come out some day, and 2). Don't ever let go of God even if people claiming to be his representatives are blowing it horridly. God is not to blame for the wrongdoing and the pain, and He can and will redeem it in our lives if we are patient. I would like them to know that *they are worthy of finding a healthy church..*' It took us a *long* time to wait for God to show us a healthy church (where we have been now for a long time), but it was worth the wait. When we stopped trying to be *members* in a denomination of our choice (the one we were in), we could focus on listening to God and watch what a healthy church looked like.

MELINDA: I wish they could know that people can be shitty. Shitty stuff happens. If, here in the Unites States the way you were treated is/was illegal, then the perpetrator should be prosecuted to the full extent of the law. I wish they could know that the strength to heal is inside them, and they are totally worth it.

KISHA: What I tell anyone who at any time feels unsafe in their faith community is two words: "Get out." I am almost never that direct regarding anything else in life, and I am extremely evasive when it comes to giving people advice. However, people's safety is of *huge* concern to me, and I will *never* be silent when it comes to protecting someone else's safety and well-being. I have a zero tolerance policy for other people's victimization to abuse and maltreatment.

DEANNA: Give yourself time. It's the worst prescription and the best one. Let yourself grieve whatever beliefs you are leaving because it is not an easy transition. Let yourself just *be.* If you can't go to church today, that's okay. If you can't open your Bible today, that's okay too. Cling to those around you who make you feel safe and loved for exactly who you are. God is in the midst of those hugs and tears, and that laughter around the dinner table. Take time to examine yourself and your heart. What triggers you? What doesn't? Where does it hurt and why? The more you can articulate this—and it sometimes can take years of work, so don't get frustrated with yourself when you can't pinpoint it overnight—the better you will be able to find a new path.

KATE: I think there is a deep need for communities of meaning. People need others they can count on. People need to be challenged to live out their values in an ever-wider circles of influence.

MARG: No one could have told me anything that would have helped for many years. But once I got sober, the best thing anyone could have said to me was what Katherine Unthank said in that workshop. In essence, "You have suffered a debilitating trauma, and your life has been forever changed by it." Almost as important, but necessarily subsequently presented, is what Nancy Hardesty would say to me later, "You are always welcome at Her table."

BILL: For people hurt by faith, there are some terribly abusive situations, and people need to get out of those. If your faith is causing you pain in any way, you should pursue things that make you feel alive and whole, as long as it is healthy not hurtful. Whatever that is, do it. When you find things that make you more whole, whatever it is, pursue that. If you are more despondent doing something, you need to be able to drop that thing. I think that applies with faith/tradition. I also understand that church/faith communities are human institutions and whatever community you find will have those same dynamics. You are going to have the same relational dynamics in your context. There will be disappointment, betrayal, and hurt anywhere. For anyone who has the courage to keep slogging through that to find a faith community, I think that is also a wonderful thing.

TO FAITH COMMUNITIES...

THE QUESTION ASKED: *What do you wish people in religion/church culture could understand about how they treat people in general and those who are wounded? How do you think they should treat people who have been wounded?*

HOPE: I wish people would understand that a little love and patience goes a long way . . . in our case, it was a case of the church deciding our son was "out of control" (He was not, but he is on the autism spectrum, and it took him *much* longer to learn things, and it was much harder for him than it was for a neurotypical child.) Had they tried to be more patient and understanding, and had they been trustworthy and respectful, things would have been so different. We wanted to stay there. We deeply grieved being kicked out, and the pain, though healed in many ways by God after 15 years, is *still* now there on some very deep levels, and I think to some extent it will be until we get to heaven where God wipes away all tears. What I wish someone from that church had told me was that the church knew the truth and was going to stand on it. Instead the people admitted to us that they were "confused" and that the "only thing we know to do is to 'submit'". So they *knew* that something stunk but went along with it. I can't do that. If I think something stinks I have to stand up and take a stand even if it costs me.

MELINDA: Listen better. Hear victims out. Listen more. Listen again. Listen until they are done telling the whole story. And then be the embodiment of empathy.

DAVID: My hope is not holding onto our scriptures rather than a person. My hope is for faith communities to be more open-minded, have a bigger mindset, and able to break out of the old paradigms—I believe thinking and feeling big can change the world. That is what I am hoping for and trying to contribute to—critiquing limiting styles in the church and helping people to be independent and interdependent. I think the mindset should be "Out with the bad and in with the good. "

KISHA: Ministry is as much about what God wants to do *in* you as it is about what He wants to do *through* you. Meanwhile, for those within religious systems who believe they can "fix" others, please stop. Physician, heal thyself. Love people where they are, receive grace for yourself, and then extend it to others. That's about all you are equipped to do, and in most unhealed circumstances, that is all that is needed: community.

FAY: Stop shooting their wounded! Listen before you speak! Be There! Cut out the cliché answers and interpretations of scripture out of context to offer words of wisdom. I wish I had been told I was loved more than their fears and their own feelings and judgments. Rebuilding and forgiveness come from admitting wrongs.

DEANNA: One thing: If you care about the doctrine more than the person, you are doing it wrong. Countless times throughout the Gospels, Jesus violated the rules in order to take care of people. I think we need to treat one another like neighbors first. Religion and doctrine come later, not the other way around. There is too much false information about other faith groups, and it is breeding fear and hate, which lead to violence. We are all on this earth here together. We are here for one another, and we need to start acting like it. I remember talking to my mother about going on a trip with an organization that helps child soldiers in Uganda. The first thing out of her mouth was, "Are they a Christian organization?" I said I didn't know for sure, but that they were doing really great work. She said that there wasn't really a point in going if they didn't share this gospel. This is a really common viewpoint by many Christians, but it is a toxic one. It says that God does not care about the basic human needs of "unbelievers." That could not be further from the truth. The God I know cares less about your rightness of theology and more about not enslaving small children. He cares more about providing water for the residents of Detroit and pulling women out of human trafficking. To *ever* suggest otherwise is to blaspheme the heart of God. (I don't often use the word "blasphemy," but I truly believe this. I don't know much, but I do know that.)

DEB: When people are representing themselves as an authority on God and Christianity, they have a lot of responsibility to their followers to make sure they are getting the right message. I wish they would realize they are playing a key part in influencing the faith of those who may not know what it is outside of that community. I have been told many times to give my pain to God. What is difficult about that is knowing that God is an all-knowing God. He knows my pain. He saw me go through it. If he wanted me to give him my pain, why would he allow me to have it in the first place? I think that communities need to realize there is true damage that can be done to someone's psyche, and the answer is not as simple as giving it up to God. Thankfully God allows us to be smart enough to have professionals who can help you on your healing journey, but mental health issues have always been dismissed as something that can be cured by having faith in God.

KATE: Well, I wish someone on the Plymouth staff had called to say goodbye instead of maintaining radio silence after I asked to be taken off their membership list. You'd think that 25 years of volunteering, financial support, leadership roles, etc., would merit a "Thank you; we're sorry to see you go." I think churches should be generous when members move on – they should find ways to express thanks and offer sincere good wishes. It hurt me when they let my husband leave without so much as a "see you around." It hurt me when they treated me the same way six months later.

JULIE: I've always been surprised people in the church and especially leaders don't want to know why you left or changed your beliefs. They don't want to hear your story. They just want to tell you how wrong/sinful you are. But then some of the people who loved and really helped us were also Christian leaders. They were a blatant exception, but I'll always be really thankful for them.

MARG: How you treat the least of your fellow human beings defines the nature of your faith. Isolating from, attacking, and denigrating LGBTQ people ruins Jesus for us and devalues the Gospel. I don't think the result of anything, any policy, or any practice, should ever be something that ruins Jesus for anyone. What can faith communities do? Recognize that LGBT people suffer from deep spiritual wounds because almost every single one of us does. For many of us, well, I'm not sure those wounds will ever fully heal; they just become part of our story. Faith communities must intentionally validate our struggle, and conscientiously participate in the efforts to challenge the views and interpretations of scripture that enable this spiritual wounding to continue. To stand by and allow this attack on an entire group of people to continue unchallenged is to implicitly demean our humanity. Faith communities must admit the reality of the trauma we have suffered at the hands of Christian people. They must recognize this has left us with special issues regarding trust, fear, and the perception of how we are being treated. They must be patient and forgiving when these issues affect how we behave. Faith communities must recognize these wounds do not heal themselves over time. They only fester. So we must be encouraged to tell our stories when we are able to do so. People of faith must listen intently to the stories of the LGBT people in their midst. Christians must admit their own part in perpetrating the injury or allowing it to happen. LGBT people may even be able to respond with authentic words of forgiveness at times. These wounds we carry will simply not heal when they are closed up and left untended. The wounds we carry must be lovingly tended to with genuine compassion. Faith communities must strive to love LGBT people with abandon and appreciate the unique voice we bring to the table.

DAVE: Every single religion that believes in a God believes in a God who creates love and structure in their lives, so why would you ever want to confuse the kids walking into your church and make them think God is anything but love and acceptance? What is the purpose of it? Don't tarnish other people's beliefs and choices. What is the purpose of doing that? All organized religions need to understand everyone may believe something a little different, and they, like us, are entitled to believe in that system. There are many disciples for many different traditions out there, and it doesn't mean one is wrong and one is right, so why don't we just keep it that way? If I like chocolate milk, and someone likes vanilla, then enjoy your milk, and I will enjoy mine. Now, strawberry milk makes me sick, but I don't go around knocking strawberry milk out of other people's hands. They are all milk, and they are all real. We can't say any one of them doesn't exist. I like religions that say, "These are my beliefs,; they don't have to be your beliefs," and are welcoming. God is about acceptance because everyone is flawed and everyone sins, and when people make a mistake, you don't want to be made to feel you are going to hell over it. I think God accepts everyone, and I want to do the same.

BILL: In my age group and demographic, a lot of people are the "nones" [spiritual but not religious] and they are leaving church. So I think whenever anyone shows up at a faith community, it should be seen as a great honor, and the community should offer hospitality rather than leaving someone to find their way. The community should have sensibilities about others. If I invited you over for dinner, and then I just sit down and start eating as you are standing there with your coat on, leaving you to figure it all out, that would not be hospitable. Or if I have a ritual at my dinner table, and I don't explain what is going to happen, that is not hospitable. I am responsible to help you land in my home. Faith communities I have been a part of have been like, "We are eating dinner and I may acknowledge you, but I'm doing my thing." For me it is all about hospitality and empathy. If you never saw football and went to the Super Bowl, your head would explode. It is all symbolic and helping people learn what the symbols and meanings are is a faith community's responsibility.

The Cracks Are Where the Light Gets In

Woundedness and Transformation

I opened this book and my story with an exploration of wounding in a Buddhist context, which led me, through hurt, back to the painful hurt from my church context. Conversely, one of the most powerfully mystic and healing experience of devout faith and human relationship came to me again through a Buddhist lens. But, if I think about it, in truth it was just through an authentically human lens.

While my basement teachings had led to a bit of a Buddhist cult, it also set me into the paradox of most of my experience of faith and faith practice. I greatly loved much of the teachings and context inherent to Buddhism and the Buddhist perspective. It resonated with the contemplative mindset I began in Buddhist teachings and then explored further in a Christian contemplative context.

After graduate school I planned a month-long solo backpacking trip to Thailand and Laos—not just because of my amorous feelings toward the Eastern philosophical lens but also due to the ease of traversing this area of the world as a single female. As was customary for my travels, I managed to get a sizeable sinus infection along my journey, so that once I made my way from Bangkok, to the northern city Chiang Mai and west to the Burmese border, I was very sick.

Boarding a plane headed for Luang Prabang, Laos, I was feeling the feverish, with sweat pouring off my brow in the tireless monsoon heat.

I found my way with a Brit and a Scot I had met on the plane to a guesthouse made of erratic plywood siding, just a block up the hill from the Mekong River. For three dollars a day and with a pounding headache, I was glad just to have a mattress and a fan. The guesthouse was owned by "Mama," or that is what she asked everyone to call her. I remember that she had a bag like Mary Poppins did, and it held everything from Band-Aids® to spare bananas, all to be offered to her guests for whatever need they might have.

As my delirium increased, and the local pharmacy did not contain the antibiotics I needed to begin to cure my illness, Mama became very concerned for my well-being. Much of my last two days in Luang Prabang was spent with Mama reaching in her bag looking for just the right aid for what ailed me.

In translation, Luang Prabang means "the Royal Buddha image," and it is a UNESCO World Heritage site both for its French colonial architecture at the city center and the abundance of Buddhist temples all throughout the city. If you are up early enough in the morning, you can see the monks seeking alms along the cobble stone streets of the town. Mama was a devout Buddhist and went to temple daily. On the day I left, headed by plane for the Southern Thailand island of Ko Tao via Ko Samui, headed toward antibiotics and beaches, Mama came into my room to say goodbye.

There are a rare few moments whose positive influence can have as deeply lasting effects and clarity as the traumatic ones. I know this from my own life and from hearing the stories of suffering for most of my professional life. This, however, was one of those positive influence moments so sacred to me that it lives as a burning exception to that rule. I remember everything about that moment, down to the temperature, sound, and lighting specific to that memory.

Mama walks in, and the fan is blowing loudly—shaking from the intensity of breeze from its perch near the ceiling. The sound was like a whizz and a thud; it was so clear because the guesthouse was otherwise nearly silent—everyone was out exploring the town. It was mid-day, but it felt like dusk in the space—the only light inside was through the spaces and slats where the plywood room walls had been nailed together unevenly.

Mama sat down on the mattress next to me; I had just finished packing my backpack for the journey.

"This morning I go to temple," she said in a little above a whisper. She took my hand and opened it with my palm facing upward.

"I get this blessed by monks. It is for help and to keep bad things away. Mama is worried about you, but this will protect."

Then she placed into my open palm a bracelet made of black oblong beads and white skulls. She closed my hand and gave it a squeeze and hugged me with such love that it filled me up with the sweet mix of joy and sadness I have only found in truly sacred moments of relationship.

I remember sitting on the plane an hour later, running my hand over my blessed bracelet now on my wrist, and beginning to well with tears I could not explain. Even in that moment, it felt potent but odd, and I remember thinking, "Why am I so sad? Why is it so hard to leave this place and this woman I only just met?"

There are those moments and those people you carry with you for a lifetime. In life and faith, in all the sweet and bittersweet moments on the rollercoaster of seeking sacredness and spirituality, there are only a handful of moments as powerful for me as those few moments with Mama in that guesthouse in Luang Prabang. Her love was so implicit and sincere. Her generosity, even with nothing to give in the tangible or economic sense, was so much more than I have received almost anywhere else. She is still one of the paragons of true faith and authentic spirituality in my life and heart. It is a rare thing—faith that pure and good.

Those are the moments. Those are the moments that beat away with love all the bad ones—from the fanatical Buddhist nun to my aggressive Catholic Monseigneur in childhood to everything in between. There is something about the purity of love that asks nothing and faith that judges no one that makes me want to believe again and again in that ineffable something greater than myself and than all the abusive examples of religion the world could ever offer.

Those are the moments that retrieve my faith in humanity and the cosmos from the hurtful and tedious evil that exists in the world. *That* is the image I want to leave you with—Mama and me in a quietly sacred moment during one summer in Laos.

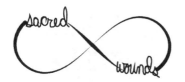

May you find your way through lonely nights.
May you find rest,
and calm and peace from sacred fights.

There are hard days. There are deep pains.
But tomorrow brings the possibility of hope,
grace, love and healing on every new horizon.

Seek the healing you deserve.
You are worth it.

ADDENDUM

Finding a Mental Health Provider
to Support Your Healing from Religious Injury,
Spiritual Abuse, and/or Church-Hurt

This is a question I get often. Since religious injury is not yet a commonly known or understood manifestation of trauma, when I speak on this issue or even on trauma in general, people ask how to access the most effective and trained provider. They want to find someone specific to religious injury, someone who will understand the unique nature of this specific hurting experience. The following are some basic tips to get you started on the road to finding a provider right for you. Even with a narrow scope like religious injury, each person may be suited to different kinds of providers, so this will vary per person in some ways, but there are some basic tips to help you on your way—regardless of your specific healing journey and fingerprint of recovery.

1. **Make sure the provider is adequately credentialed and certified in counseling.** You want to make sure he or she is a master's level clinician or above in a field of therapy or counseling. The major fields of clinical therapy practice include psychology, psychiatry (although psychiatrists are usually medical doctors whose main function is prescribing mental health medication; a select few provide counseling), social work, marriage and family therapy, counseling psychology, and mental health counseling. Also make sure he or she is licensed in the state he or she practices

in. You can also check the record of every licensed professional in your state through the state's licensing website to make sure the licensure status is in good standing—meaning, there are no any pending charges for issues related to client care.

2. **Check to see if his or her Psychology Today profile and/ or website lists trauma and PTSD as one of the areas of specialty.** This does not guarantee he or she is an expert in traumatology, but if it is referenced, there is a better chance he or she has a minimal working knowledge of trauma. It is good to know not everyone who mentions trauma in their therapy biographical information is a trauma expert—many may have a generalist's ability to treat trauma, and many will not have any direct practice with religious injury and spiritual abuse as an area of practice. This doesn't mean this is not a good fit for you—it is just important to go into your consultation with a provider with a reasonable expectation of his or her abilities and knowledge about religious-oriented trauma.

3. **Imagine your first session with a provider as a job interview for that person.** You have no obligation to commit to a provider just because he or she has met with you—you are the person who decides what is best for your care. Trauma survivors tend to be "yes" people as a method of self-protection, but you need to know you have the option of choice here. Have a list of questions you want to ask. A few sample questions are: How much of your practice involves treating trauma and PTSD as the primary diagnosis? How many years have you been treating trauma? What therapeutic interventions do you use specifically for traumatic stress? Have you had any experience with religious trauma/injury specifically? If so, in what way? How do you treat religious injury and spiritual abuse? Are there any differences between treating this trauma and other traumas? How comfortable are you with addressing this issue in counseling?

4. **Find resources outside of your local area.** While you might find a therapist who is a good fit in your area, it may be unlikely he or she has extensive experience with religious injury or traumatic experience. What can supplement that gap can be accessing resources, which are outside of your local resources—books, websites, online religious hurt forums, and specialists.

5. **You can then bring some of these resources to your chosen therapy provider.** If they are both adept and humble, they will be willing to learn along with you and process some of the elements unique to this kind of traumatic stress. No therapist will know everything, but a willingness to learn and grow with you is crucial. If a provider does this, then he or she is also that much more equipped to deal with this issue with future clients.

6. **Know this field is growing.** Although trauma experts and trauma experts who also understand religious injury may be limited at present, both of the fields are growing in notice and practice due to necessity. The resources and providers available, as well as other programming for healing—retreats, conferences, gatherings, etc.—will only continue to grow. Find what serves you best in the present moment and know that it is an ever-expanding area of study and practice.

Lightning Source UK Ltd.
Milton Keynes UK
UKOW06f1933270616

277201UK00019B/858/P